T0191048

Public Philosophy and Patriotism

Other Books of Interest from St. Augustine's Press

Public Philosophy and Patriotism
Essays on the Declaration and Us
PAUL SEATON

ST. AUGUSTINE'S PRESS
South Bend, Indiana

Manufactured in the United States of America.

1 2 3 4 5 6   29 28 27 26 25 24

Library of Congress Control Number: 2024939224

Paperback ISBN: 978-1-58731-943-3
Ebook ISBN: 978-1-58731-944-0

∞ The paper used in this publication meets the minimum
requirements of the American National Standard for Information Sciences –
Permanence of Paper for Printed Materials, ANSI Z39.48-1984.

St. Augustine's Press
www.staugustine.net

TABLE OF CONTENTS

To Diana and Lauren,
Amicīs carissimīs,
Magnas et multas gratias.

INTRODUCTION

Inspired by a marvelous combination of filial piety and maternal wisdom, America commemorates her birthday each year on the Fourth of July. Annually on that resonant date, she would have us look back (and up) in gratitude, then forward with renewed purpose. The soul of America is somehow concentrated in this civic celebration. And central to the celebration, central to the commemoration, is the Declaration of Independence. The Declaration is the self-conscious expression of the self-conscious launch of a new country. Some of us still read it out loud at our public and private celebrations of the day.

But along with the patriotic idealism to which I just gave voice, the Declaration has fallen on hard times. Its luster has been dimmed, its credibility regularly challenged. (The New York Times' *1619 Project*, which attempts to replace 1776 with 1619 as the true founding of America—a thoroughly racist America—can stand for a legion of such endeavors.[1]) The essays that follow were penned in an effort to help restore the Declaration's luster and credibility and to demonstrate its relevance to us today. In the midst of the

---

1   For two telling critiques of the 1619 Project, see Peter W. Wood, *1620: A Critical Response to the 1619 Project* (Encounter Books, 2020), and Phillip W. Magness, *The 1619 Project: A Critique* (American Institute for Economic Research, 2020). For Lincoln's engagement with the relationship between 1619 and 1776, see Diana Schaub, *His Greatest Speeches: How Lincoln Moved the Nation* (St. Martin's Press, 2021), Chapter 3, "The Second Inaugural: 1619 and Charity for All": "The Second Inaugural is the original and better 1619 Project" (p. 110).

celebrations, the denigrations, and the hot dogs, precious little attention is paid to the document itself. Sometimes displayed like a civic relic, sometimes a few famous phrases intoned, it's not often taken seriously as an argument, much less as a possible guide to today. However, as a longtime teacher, I constantly discovered that students become fascinated by the text when they actually had to read it. There is so much more there than they had been led to believe. My classroom teaching and experience is the foundation of this collection.

Then friends moved it along. My dear friend Diana Schaub, herself a superb student of the American founding, African American thought, Lincoln, and much more, was always receptive to my thoughts on the Declaration. She solicited my class notes and would encourage me with "These are great! You should write these up." She planted the seed.

Next came Lauren Weiner, Richard Reinsch, and Brian Smith, all at the fine website *Law and Liberty*. Lauren, another dear friend, brought me into the stable of writers for the website in early 2014 and oversaw my first essays on the Declaration. When she moved on, Richard kindly allowed the tradition to continue, and when he too moved on, so did his successor, Brian. To all, I am most grateful.[2]

Then came the final nudge. It was administered by two other friends, Carl Eric Scott and Titus Techera. Over the years, they made a point of writing me after each essay appeared and commenting on it. And at a certain point, they also started telling me, "You should work these into a book." Now there were several friendly voices encouraging me.

So, after a recent effort, "Government Under Judgment," I sat down and pulled together what I had written on the Declaration

---

2   Brian Smith in particular graciously permitted the reprinting of these essays which originally appeared on the *Law and Liberty* website.

over the years for *Law and Liberty*. My friends were right! I indeed had a book. So, again, my thanks to them all. (The usual disclaimer applies: nothing I say should be charged to their accounts. I am fully capable of making my own mistakes in interpretation and application.)

*

The foregoing account of the genesis of this collection of essays was intended to serve purposes beyond the grateful acknowledgement of debts. It also indicates important features of the essays (and two book reviews) collected here. Given their original venue, there were space limitations to attend to, as well as a diverse readership to consider. The first meant that I had to be straightforward, often lapidary, the second that the essays had to appeal to a variety of political views—or at least not immediately trigger them. All that was fine with me and the initial essays toed the line by being largely expository. Aware of our partisan differences, I tried to recall the Declaration as Americans' common patrimony.

I continued in that vein even into the beginning of the Trump era, when Donald Trump appeared as a candidate for the presidency. Given the charges and countercharges exchanged between candidate Trump and candidate Clinton, each accusing the other of despotic inclinations and intentions, I sketched the Declaration's portrait of a despot and the checklist it provides to detect one in action or aspiration. This was an attempt to interject some Declaration objectivity into the partisan hysteria. Similarly, I attempted a reconciliation of the vision of justice held by proponents of identity politics with the traditional American view expressed in the Declaration. Admittedly, this was something of a Hail Mary pass. But the "hopeful" aim of the essays was to invite partisans to repair to common standards and to seek a certain measure of reconciliation.

Even when, immediately after Trump's election, a self-proclaimed

"Resistance" declared itself foursquare against him, I surveyed the Declaration for criteria that the Resistance would have to follow to legitimate itself and that others could use to judge its legitimacy and activities. But that essay, "Resistance in the Light of 1776," also became the start of a significant turn in the essays. This came about because of the venue in which the essays first appeared.

In those years, *Law and Liberty* had comboxes, so readers could share their judgments and their thoughts. This particular essay provoked an unusual amount of comments. I initially tried to respond to them, but the volume became too much. So I asked Richard Reinsch if I could explain more fully my view of the identity politics espoused by the Resistance in some follow-up pieces. He said yes. Then followed six essays in the span of one month (August 2017). After that lengthy critical exposition, identity politics—a toxic mixture of race- and gender-obsessed ideology, tendentious and often false history, economics, and sociology, and a nefarious inversion of the moral and spiritual orders[3]—publicly became a negative norm for me. It must be battled on every front. *Politica identica delenda est.*

This meant that when its proponents moved from Resistance to Power in the Biden administration, my focus and application of the Declaration shifted accordingly. "The Declaration's Principled 'We'" sought for guidance for those of a mind to resist the ascendant Resistance. What kind of "We" would the Declaration

---

3   In addition to the authors and texts referenced in the essays, the reader interested in the topic of identity politics—early on popularly styled "political correctness," later known as "wokeness" or "cultural Marxism"—should read Joshua Mitchell's elegantly written *American Awakening: Identity Politics and Other Afflictions of Our Time* (Encounter Books, 2020); James Lindsay's turgidly written *Race Marxism* (New Discourses, 2022); and Christopher Rufo's well-written *America's Cultural Revolution* (Broadside Books, 2023). Mitchell's book has the special virtue of highlighting the spiritual inversion, the garbling of Christian categories, inherent in the ideology.

recommend we be? As it happens, the essay resonated and I was asked to appear on a national podcast to discuss the essay and it was also picked up by two prominent websites for dissemination. There was, it appeared, a "We" to be formed. The last essay in the collection, "Government Under Judgment," restates and updates the underlying thesis of the essays: In the Declaration's view of things, government is erected to serve a free people, not the other way around. Today, when we are threatened by new and daunting forms of despotism: identity politics or "wokeness" and what Aaron Kheriaty calls "the biomedical security state," we do well to repair to this teaching and the example of our forebears who first fought against encroaching despotism.

*

The title of this collection is *Public Philosophy and Patriotism: The Declaration and Us.* "Public philosophy" is a cousin to "political philosophy" and both are found in the essays. The title aims at putting before the reader the four elements that form the dialectical coordinates of the essays, with their various possibilities of being related and compared. The Declaration is the chief pole, to which the others are related. Quite remarkably, it combines public philosophy and patriotism. That is, it presents a mind formed by political philosophy (and theology), acting quite thoughtfully and dramatically on the basis of those ideas and on their behalf. The first task of these essays was to draw out the ideas and, equally, the agent.

Then, the ideas and model needed to be applied to our contemporary circumstances and debates. Above, I sketched the itinerary I took, a combination of logical development and responding to contemporary events. Throughout, understanding the Declaration and applying it to us was the common thread. But two things came more and more to the fore.

On one hand, the reality of partisanship. As our politics became more polarized and partisan, the essays had to address that massive fact. They did so in three ways and three phases (irenic; exploratory; opposition), ending with the Declaration being deployed to oppose what would entail the death of anything approaching the vision of America limned by the Declaration. Thus three of the essays in this collection are explicitly my own "partisan" contribution to keeping the spirit of '76 alive.[4]

On the other hand, our increasingly troubled situation called for greater use of political philosophy than is found in the Declaration. Hence the introduction of classical political philosophers such as Socrates and Aristotle and contemporary ones like Pierre Manent into the discussion. As the reader will discover, these eminent thinkers help us take the measure of our partisan divides. More positively, they provide precious substantive content to the "thought" in "thoughtful citizenship" that the title of the first essay brings to the reader's attention. Indeed, I placed "public philosophy" before "patriotism" in the title of this collection in order to indicate that the Declaration's model of citizenship and agency— its patriotism—follows from a form of thinking.

*

I conclude with a few truth-in-advertising comments. The order of the chapters is largely, but not entirely, the chronological order in which the essays appeared. I have changed the order of five of the essays in order to make for a more logical order, one more intelligible to the reader. In order to help navigate the resulting difference between the original and new order, each essay is prefaced by

4   Chapter Three, "The Declaration's Civic Anthropology"; Chapter Fifteen, "The Declaration's Principled 'We'"; and Chapter Sixteen, "Government Under Judgment."

a short statement of its original context and intent. I also made a few deletions and a number of additions to the originals. The deletions were to avoid repetition, the additions usually to clarify or expand an already existing thought. From time to time, I updated a point with a contemporary reference or comment. I was struck in rereading the essays how well they tracked then-contemporary events and now make comprehensible events that followed, e.g., the Left's vitriolic reaction to *Dobbs* and the Biden administration's ongoing promotion of woke progressivism. That gave me some reassurance of their validity. It remains to the reader, of course, to judge their success in expositing and applying the Declaration to us.

Paul Seaton
April 18, 2024

Chapter One

Several considerations guided my inaugural essay on the Declaration. For the occasion, I needed to convey a certain persona, in the essay, to strike an appropriate tone. Given that the essay was inaugural, it also needed to establish a framework. The persona adopted was that of a thoughtful citizen, a reflective patriot. The tone, a magisterial one, which expressed respect, even admiration, for the document, but a desire to probe it as well. Jefferson's famous phrase describing the character of the document—"an expression of the American mind"—gave me my hook and my theme: What kind of mind was the American mind?

THE DECLARATION AND THOUGHTFUL CITIZENSHIP (2014)

If democracy is to endure, thoughtful citizenship is a requirement for a critical mass of the citizenry. We have an opportunity to live up to that obligation today. America's birthday offers an opportunity to go back to the self-conscious beginnings of our common enterprise, where we meet the Declaration of Independence.

In a letter to Richard Henry Lee, Jefferson famously characterized the Declaration as "an expression of the American mind." Let's spend a few minutes considering that mind. We will find it to be: 1) logical; 2) liberty-loving; 3) manly; and 4) gesturing towards, and calling for, philosophical and theological reflection.

In other words, it is quite an impressive mind. We have a lot to live up to.

The Declaration's Basic Structure and Argument

The Declaration nicely divides into five parts:

A preamble announcing the purpose of the document;
A statement of principles of politics, principles of political evaluation and of political construction;
A list of twenty-seven grievances against the Crown and Parliament, "injuries and usurpations" effected by the metropole, chiefly the king;
A brief reference to the repeated efforts at redress by the colonists, all, alas, without success; and, finally,
The logical conclusion of the foregoing.

Given these principles of political right, given these facts—that is, the misdeeds of king and parliament which evince a settled design of despotic ambition—it is the colonists' right, it is their duty, to determine that they will not acquiesce in their own subjection, but declare their independence as a people. They are warranted in this bold act by "the laws of nature and of Nature's God."

A Logical Mind

Much could be said, in terms of matter and form, about the Declaration's display of logical thinking. One central point will have to suffice. Perhaps most remarkable is the confidence it shows in the power of reasoning. Subjects not always deemed to be amenable to rational analysis and determination— political right order, tyranny, and revolution—find themselves directly and coherently dealt with. To be sure, doing so requires a variety of reason's activities: the articulation of principles, the discernment of relevant facts, inferring causes from effects, knitting together ends and means.

The Declaration does all this and more despite the highly fraught and even belligerent situation that brought it about.[5] Its confidence in the ability of reason to understand and guide politics, including revolutionary activity, is so remarkable that one could raise it up as a model of capacious political reflection, effective rhetoric, and deliberate action. The Framers of the Constitution and Abraham Lincoln certainly did. Why not Americans today?

A Liberty-Loving, Manly Mind

To be sure, the Declaration's mind is not merely logical, not simply cerebral. All this thinking is at the service of something else: in a word, of liberty, both individual and collective. And liberty, while Nature's and God's gift and humanity's birthright, needs to be loved as well as understood, and sometimes defended with life and fortune. The Declaration's argument is motivated by just such a spirited love.

Hence the need for "manliness" on the part of liberty-lovers. After giving the argument for independence on behalf of "the good People of these colonies," the fifty-five representatives pledge to one another their lives, fortunes, and sacred honor. They are willing to risk everything for the justness of their cause. Liberty is worth these sacrifices. In so risking, they insert themselves into an ongoing history of the defense of liberty in the colonies, one that is limned in the text itself. Earlier legislatures, it says, had resisted "with manly firmness" the Crown's encroachments. Now it is their turn, and they find inspiration in the stout character and actions of their predecessors.

This points to the dramatic character of the Declaration. It

5   "Belligerent" comes from *bellum-gerere*, to wage war. The Declaration provides a list of belligerent actions by the Crown in its last four "injuries and usurpations."

self-consciously casts its composers and signers as *dramatis personae*, as participants in a mighty contest between encroaching tyranny and lovers of liberty. Both parties—tyrants and throwers-off of tyranny—exhibit relevant character traits and the text is not shy about using a language of virtue and vice. One might even be moved to see the Declaration as the first epic poem that Americans penned about themselves.

Toward Philosophy and Theology

One last trait identified above, "philosophical and theological reflection," remains to be considered. The mind at work in the Declaration is, to coin an awkward phrase, "assertively comprehensive"—or even, although it too is a bit awkward—"philosophical-theological lite." I hasten to explain.

On one hand, its vision is comprehensive. It includes articulations of God (four references to the Deity); of Nature or "the world"; of "all men" or human beings; of government (its origins, ends, and proper structure); of "the course of human events" (history); and the fundamental distinction between civilization and barbarism. And it exhibits an awareness and concern for the opinions of contemporary mankind. In other words, it is a mind with high, deep, and broad vistas.

Yet its fundamental views are, for the most part, merely asserted. For example, God is asserted or "declared," but not argued for. His existence and nature and activities are premises of a further argument, not the subjects of inquiry or demonstration. The same is true for the principles of politics in the second part of the document.

This is not to say that arguments could not be given to support the assertions. Their absence, however, does tell us something more about the character of the Declaration. It is a practical document with important theoretical content. It wants to reason and argue, but its argument's purpose is primarily practical: to declare the causes that impel separation. A thoughtful reader should acknowledge the Declaration's practical aim, as well as ask: what philosophical and theological arguments were implied, or need to be supplied, to justify its assertions?

Today's American Study

On the 238th anniversary of this founding document, therefore, perhaps a distinctive sort of "American Studies" is in order. Americans could sit down and reread it with due attention. They could consider its explicit words and claims, as well as the concepts and argument they convey. Encountering what it explicitly says, they could speculate about its missing premises and arguments. To be true to the text and guided by it, this reflection would take cognizance of the obvious structure, purpose, and meaning of the document.

If this happened, the first and current generations of independent Americans would be thoughtfully connected. Not only that, we today would be exercising two American virtues: filial gratitude and intellectual independence. That would make for a very fine Fourth of July.

Chapter Two

With the initial articulation of the American mind in place, it was possible, and it was necessary, to fill it in. What must first be added to the picture practically imposed itself: the Declaration's principles of politics. For one of the most important lessons of the document was that politics not only could be rationally thought about, but that they could be rationally guided and determined. The Declaration conveyed principles that made possible the evaluation of actual politics and the construction of a "Form of Government" that would allow free and reasonable politics to be conducted. What was quite remarkable was that these lessons were taught in the midst of the most stressful of circumstances. How could we today, in less fraught circumstances, fail to consider the example and the lessons?

THE DECLARATION'S PRINCIPLES OF POLITICS (2015)

Last year I penned an analysis and something of a paean to the Declaration of Independence. Perhaps a follow-up is in order. Who knows, perhaps it could become a Fourth of July tradition? Certainly there is a good deal more in the famous text than one reading could convey. In fact, the general purpose of this one is to provide material for reflection. That would be a thoughtful way of being patriotic on this day of commemoration and celebration.

Principles, Principally Political

As we saw last year, the Declaration applies various sorts of principles—theological; anthropological; and political—to a set of "Facts," chiefly "injuries and usurpations" on the part of the British monarch (and, belatedly, Parliament). It judges the facts as evincing a design of tyranny, and concludes, as it began, with the necessity and duty of revolution and independence, understood as self-government by and for free men and women. With quite recent events in mind (concerning state power and civil liberties), it is fitting to look at some of what I style "the principles of politics" enunciated in the document. They can be found in three distinct parts of the text: the statement of principles that begins "We hold these truths to be self-evident"; in the list of twenty-seven "injuries and usurpations" that forms the third part of the text; and in the final part, where the colonies declare themselves to be *de facto* and *de jure* "Free and Independent States" and some of their important "Power[s]" as states are enumerated.

Each part provides important statements concerning the principles of politics, that is, the ends and means, necessary and/or desirable, of political activity, especially in the formation of government. The first introduces the important term "principles"; the list of grievances points to the right order of government and governmental action by indicting the negative actions of the King and Parliament: "injuries" means a violation ("in-") of what is right or just ("*jus/juris*"); while "usurpations" implies authority transgressing rightful limits. The last section picks up the introduction of "the State" in the third part, as well as the affirmation that government is essentially a matter of organized "powers" in the second section, and lists four powers that States possess, adding to those previously indicated.[6]

6   "[A]s Free and Independent States, they have full Power to levy War, conclude Peace, contract Alliances, establish Commerce, and to do

14

Dual (and Dueling) Purposes

In good teleological fashion, it is appropriate to begin with the Declaration's express statements of the purposes of government. Please note the plurals: "statements" and "purposes." Everyone, so to speak, knows that the Declaration maintains that, in its normative view, "Governments are instituted" "to secure these rights" (that is, "unalienable rights," "Creator"-endowed rights, "among which are life, liberty, and the pursuit of happiness"). But attention is hardly ever given to a closely following statement: "whenever any Form of Government becomes destructive of these ends [the aforementioned unalienable rights], it is the Right of the People to alter or abolish it, and to institute new Government, laying its foundation on such principles and organizing its powers in such form, as to them shall seem most likely to effect their Safety and Happiness."[7] This last phrase—"to effect their Safety and Happiness"— is an additional statement of governmental purpose, one that envisages the People as such, as a whole, and not just discrete individuals and their rights. Moreover, now the end of government is two-fold: "Safety and Happiness."

Apropos to these additions, I restrict myself to two comments. 1) The phrase "Safety and Happiness" indicates the alpha and the

all other Acts and Things which Independent States may of right do."

7   *Nota bene*: the very phrase in which individual rights are presented as "ends" of government indicates that "rights" cannot be limited to those that individuals possess. It speaks of "the Right of the People to alter or abolish" unsuitable Government. Similarly, later in the bill of indictments, the Declaration speaks of "the right of Representation in the Legislature, a right inestimable to them and formidable to tyrants only." The protection of rights is not limited to individual rights. Hence the need to focus on the Declaration's presentation of "the People" who also have rights, as I do above.

omega of collective existence, its pediment in safety or security and a people's ultimate aspirations toward collective fulfillment and achievement. That these two are not the same, that they do not always cohere, that they are left open for determination, render them intrinsically questionable and permanently debatable. Americans, both in government and without, will always have these goals to clarify and decisions to make concerning their content and relations.

2) This complexity or ambiguity is only increased when one recalls the original statement of governmental purpose, the protection or security of unalienable rights. It did not take recent NSA debates to know that individual rights and public safety can be in tension, nor much imagination to come up with tensions, real or claimed, between visions or projects of collective betterment and individual rights.

In short, the goals of government recognized by the Declaration set up a system in which a never-ending debate will take place between, let's say, a more liberal or libertarian emphasis on individual rights and a more democratic accent on popular or collective ends. It would be interesting, likely illuminating, to survey American political history through this lens. However that survey may turn out, the goals of government according to the Declaration are complex, not simple (nor straightforward), and it is reductionistic to simply affirm the rights-protection purpose, although it was stated first and is essential. Nor for that matter should collective goals, whether low and solid or high and enriching, be proposed or pursued without consideration of individual, and individuals', rights. With deliberate paradox, one could call this the first American "debatable consensus." There are others, and the Declaration limns them as well.

How to Form (Our) Government?

Government, we were told above, is a matter of "principles" and "powers," "foundation" and "form"—eventuating in a "Form of Government." In this view, government is a human construct, with intelligence laying its "foundation" on yet deeper "principles," then thoughtfully "organizing" its "just powers," the whole forming a structure that can effectively pursue the ends for which it is formed, while guarding against the great temptation of power, tyranny. (Incompetence does not seem to be a concern.) The most basic powers appear clearly in the section devoted to British misdeeds; they are the well-known legislative, executive, and judicial powers of classical liberalism. And many principles of the construction of government are stated or implied throughout: the subordination of military to civilian authority is one; the independence of the judiciary another. The primacy of the legislative power and of legislation is indicated by their precedence in the bill of indictments.

Thus, the Declaration limns what we could call a political science of government, that is, of the just and artful construction of government. (The distinction between political philosophy and political science I employ is found in Locke.) This does not mean that all questions of governmental formation are addressed, much less answered, by the document. The fact that the same Congress that ratified the Declaration also approved the Articles of Confederation would indicate that there was still considerable reflection to be done in this regard, including the meaning and application of principles already accepted.[8]

The Declaration's Core Conviction

Still, a basic point remains: the American mind which produced and ratified the Declaration believed that government could be thought about in a principled (i.e., non-partisan) way, and that the fundamental distinction between tyrannical and free government was accessible to those who grasped the relevant principles of its construction and operation and could judge facts in

8   See Chapter Five for more on this topic.

their light. A reconsideration and revivification of that belief would be a worthy goal and result of today's commemoration. *Libertas semper vigilans, semper judicans.*

Chapter Three

This and the following essay are the first of the essays that have been relocated from their original chronological order. This has been done to respect a logical order. In the previous essay, I wrote: "The Declaration applies various sorts of principles—theological, anthropological, and political—to a set of "Facts"—chiefly "injuries and usurpations" on the part of the British monarch (and, belatedly, Parliament)." After the political principles, it is necessary to treat the anthropological and theological principles. With them, we have a solid foundation.

However, in writing, context matters, and the original context for this essay was America three years into the Biden administration and just having been released from the authoritarianism of the pandemic response. That draconian response showed those who have eyes to see just how parlous our times are, how nefarious and powerful the enemies of American liberal democracy are. (On this one should read Aaron Kheriaty's *The New Abnormal*, mentioned in the text. I reviewed it at: https://lawliberty.org/book-review/confronting-pandemic-tyranny/.) This "apocalyptic" (i.e., revelatory) context called for a treatment that was not just enlightening, but encouraging and empowering. Hence its focus on agency.

THE DECLARATION'S CIVIC ANTHROPOLOGY (2023)

It is the Fourth of July, so it is time for a Law and Liberty tradition: a "Declaration and Us" essay. Begun in 2014, these essays attempt to extract nuggets of political wisdom from the founding document of the United States and apply them to today's political controversies. The two operations are premised on the belief that the Declaration contains perennial wisdom—wisdom that can not only guide but also judge us Americans today. A bold claim, it echoes the bold claim to revolutionary independence on the basis of permanent principles made in the document itself.

Contending Civic Anthropologies

This year I plan to talk about a topic I have not talked about before: the civic anthropology of the Declaration. (What I mean by the phrase will become clear in due course.) This choice of topic is prompted by what I think is one of the basic issues that our current circumstances compel us to think about: what is human nature? This, of course, is a major topic of dispute today; one only needs to write the word "transgender." In keeping with the Declaration's *political* focus and emphasis, however, I will not say anything about the Declaration on human sexuality other than to note that it includes the "Sexes" (along with "Ages" and "Conditions") in a list of items that should be treated in a discriminating way in civilized warfare.[9]

What I have in mind is the issue of civic anthropology that was raised in dramatic fashion the past two years by the draconian "Covid-justified" measures—lockdowns, school shutdowns, required vaccinations, vaccine passports, masks, social distancing, etc.—imposed on the public. Clearly these measures presupposed a distinctive view of the members of democratic society. They were viewed in the aggregate, not as individuals, and as threatened (and threatening) bodies, not souls (public worship was not deemed an

---

9   The events of October 7, 2023, showed the contemporary relevance
     of this teaching.

"essential service"). Many were shamed, frightened, and coerced into submitting to their putative scientific betters and political superiors. What we could call old-fashioned democratic dignity involving the rights of conscience and a panoply of civil and constitutional rights was deliberately and cruelly denied. If we are to avoid a replay of this authoritarian scenario, we need to unmask the perpetrators' ideology, power centers, and networks, and revive the sources of democratic dignity. Thinkers like Giorgio Agamben and Aaron Kheriaty have contributed importantly to the first task with their analyses of "the biomedical security state." As for the second task, we can take today's celebration as an opportunity to reconsider the civic self-understanding of our forebears who successfully resisted encroaching despotism. Fundamental to it was a distinctive understanding—a normative understanding—of what it is to be a human being.

"We Hold These Truths" in Context

When it comes to the Declaration's notion of human nature, most will turn instinctively to its second section, what I have previously called its "principles of politics." There we find the most famous lines of the document: "We hold these truths to be self-evident, that all men are created equal, that they are endowed by their Creator with certain unalienable Rights, that among these are Life, Liberty and the pursuit of Happiness." These lines are indeed a good starting point for what the Declaration has to say about man but, following an old interpretive principle, they need to be read in the light of the nature and purpose of the document as a whole. This allows us to see new dimensions of meaning in the familiar words, dimensions of which we are in particular need today.

The tendency is to read them as a detached "theoretical" affirmation. Now, I would be the last to deny that reading them in this way has yielded insights (as well as generated scholarly contro-versy). I did so myself in an earlier chapter. However, as I also said previously, the Declaration is not a theoretical document; it is very much a practical document, and it employs the phrases cited above in an account of its *deliberation* and *decision* to act a certain way. The lines, therefore, need to be taken contextually in a more prac-tical, or active, manner, and not simply as a statement of fact or belief. The Declaration looks at "all men," or human nature, in the light of its own (and others') purposive activity and activity's norms. Looking at them in a practical light and out of a practical concern, it perforce discovers a correlative object: human beings as agents.

This is subtly conveyed in a word twice repeated in the passage: "created/Creator." The act that creates "all men"—"creation" it-self—is an act, a supreme act, and its object here, "all men," par-takes in that dynamism. In and by their creation, men are equipped with powers of action and norms of action. Thus, to the explicit descriptors concerning "all men" conveyed in the lines—created equal, endowed with unalienable rights—the Declaration's practi-cal perspective would have us add: made for action, made for right action.

Today it is important to highlight this practical aspect of the Declaration's teaching about man because of our situation and the challenges we face. It is important to emphasize our capacity for agency, our nature as agents, because our world is so complex and the challenges we face so daunting, that many run the risk of retreat-ing or capitulating before the complexities and the challenges. To go forward as free citizens we need a sense, nay the conviction, of our nature and capacities as agents. For example, in the face of an edu-cational system that divides citizens into victims and victimizers, we need an education not just in human and civic equality but in agency and its proper use. This, the Declaration itself provides in several ways.

Embodied Universals

Thus, after laying this principled foundation, it brings it to bear on a determinate set of agents, the king and his allies in parliament and the "good People of these Colonies" and their eminent "Representatives." The Declaration is both a narrative and a denouement of a grand contest between particular lovers of liberty and those who would deny it to them. Its focus on their dramatic back-and-forth in subsequent parts of the document should not, however, cause us to lose sight of the anthropological universals being applied to the dueling particulars. The latter embody and are judged in their light. And as we have begun to see, these universals are both ontological and moral.

"Unalienable"

In this connection, I draw the reader's attention to another word in the passage: "unalienable." It contains a most important implication. It implies that a being—in this case, a human being—has a definite structure and composition. Taking one element out of it (in this case, rights) entails the destruction of the being. "Unalienable" means that without the feature, the thing as a distinct kind does not exist, conceptually or really. By it, the Declaration signals its belief in a fixed human nature. To be sure, this is a matter of implication, of brief indication. Nonetheless, with certain "unalienable" items ascribed to "all men" as part of their native "endowment," we are encouraged to pursue a certain line of reflection: What else is unalienable in human nature?

Performative Rationality

Reason comes immediately to mind. To see it in its Declaration richness, however, its *normative* richness, another characteristic of the document must be taken into account: its *performative enactment* of its view of human nature. What the Declaration has to say about human nature's faculty of reason is displayed *in deed*, rather than "theorized" in it. The great act of reason which is the Declaration itself combines, in a focused synthesis, a number of distinctly rational categories and operations: the grasp of "principles," a survey of "Facts" that connects effects to causes, self-reflection and moral judgment (on self and other), the determinations of "Prudence," and more. The Declaration affirms reason's amplitude precisely by exercising its range.

Connecting the Dots Today

This full panoply of reason is still available to American citizens and no doubt is required to consider the recent "Covid-justified" (sic) authoritarianism. Many dots need to be connected, both at home and abroad, to have an understanding of the networks of causes, triggers, and beneficiaries of a worldwide pandemic, responded to in draconian anti-democratic ways that were planned, prepared, and even "war-gamed" by powerful individuals and groups, as Aaron Kheriaty details in his book, *The New Abnormal*, especially in a 14-page section entitled "War-Gaming Pandemics." After laying out a series of "simulation exercises" undertaken by "intelligence and other government agencies in the United States" beginning in 1999, he writes that "this series of pandemic war games culminated in an astonishing simulation exercise, which preceded the first publicly reported case of Covid by only a few weeks." The beginning of his discussion deserves citing, in part because of the cast of characters it introduces:

> In October 2019 the renamed Johns Hopkins Center for Health Security, in partnership with the World Economic Forum and the Bill & Melinda Gates Foundation

organized a tabletop pandemic simulation scenario with epidemiologists and other experts called "Event 201: A Global Pandemic Exercise." Participants included high-ranking individuals from the World Bank, the World Economic Forum, the Chinese government, the world's largest pharmaceutical company (Johnson & Johnson), the CDC, a former NSA/CIA director, and Avril Haynes, later tapped by [President] Biden to be the director of national intelligence—the highest-level intelligence official in the United States. Several of the participants in this simulation quickly moved into key positions to run our real covid pandemic response only a few months later.

Like all its predecessors, "[t]he pandemic exercise culminate[d] in a compulsory mass vaccination campaign, during which the … participants strategize[d] about how to use censorship and other authoritarian measures to silence recalcitrant dissidents." "War-gaming" is indeed the appropriate word here, but it must be extended to a war conducted by an administration and its allies, domestic and foreign, against its own citizens.

Kheriaty's 262-page book is chock-full of such public domain facts. The Declaration can provide the rational categories and operations required to come to grips with them, as well as those the reader may collect on his or her own.

Prudence's Delicate Task

It also cautions that the time to do so is not indefinite or infinite, that at some point defending our liberties against those who wish liberal democracy ill will confront the conjoined imperatives of "Necessity," "Right," and "Duty." Then the stark alternatives before freedom will be imminently present. In a countervailing way, however, it also reminds those more advanced than their fellow citizens in this complex investigation, of the need for patience with them, given the long-suffering character of the populace before political evils, as well as the unprecedented character of our situation, where most established points of orientation have proven inadequate. Prudence alone can dictate how to navigate these realities.

At least one thing is sure: "Facts" must be constantly sought out and marshalled and their despotic "Design" repeatedly laid out in public and private. I would venture that this is the first task of those who today would fulfill the role of "Representatives" as the Declaration presents the type. This can be done by those in government, such as Congressional oversight committees, and those not in the government, such as the Brownstone Institute or the indomitable Kheriaty.[10]

Two Necessary Kinds of Firmness

Of course, human nature is more than reason and the Declaration's civic-minded anthropology is more than reason detecting and denouncing advancing tyranny. In the Declaration's own terminology, it is also an expression of "manly Firmness," as well as of various cardinal virtues. (We invoked prudence above.) These moral categories are another indication that the Declaration presupposes a fixed view of human nature: only on such a basis can it discern, name, praise, and blame positive and negative developments of that nature. In the Declaration's judging eyes, while all human beings are created equal, not all human conduct, not all moral characters, are created equal. There are villains and heroes in the Declaration's narrative of the contest over liberty and self-government and these are starkly contrasted in both moral ("Justice and Magnanimity," "Cruelty," "Perfidy") and political

10   https://brownstone.org/. https://substack.com/@aaronkheriaty.

terms ("free People," "Tyrant"). Those (progressives, libertarians) who only take from the Declaration the thought that human beings are equal and free, and go on to claim that it thereby provides license for radically egalitarian self-definition, fail to see the created rational substance that undergirds human equality and freedom and turn a blind eye to the moral categories rooted in it that the Declaration freely employs.

Among these qualities, two stand out as ones we arguably are most in need of today: manliness and trust in God, or as the Declaration phrases them: "manly Firmness" and "firm Reliance on the Protection of divine Providence." Like our forebears, our efforts at "humble" "petitions" for "Redress" have been largely ignored or scorned by unrepentant would-be Masters; sterner virtues are therefore needed to steel those who wish to defend their civil and political liberties and, more deeply, their God-given natural rights. But because the task is so daunting, powers beyond our own, as well as greater than those of our powerful enemies, need to be found. The Declaration itself, which begins with the affirmation of Creator-endowed natural rights and ends with a firm reliance on divine Providence, instructs us where to look.

Chapter Four

The following essay is the second to depart from the chronological order in which it appeared. It completes our treatment of "principles." To invoke an Aristotelian distinction: while not "first for us," theological principles are "first in themselves," dealing as they do with the first Principle, both in itself and in its relationship to the world and man. In this limited but important sense, the Declaration is Aristotelian.

Besides its topic, one other feature distinguished this essay from its predecessors. In it, I began with a contemporary controversy. It occurred between two battling conservatives, one of whom invoked the Declaration as a litmus test of American conservatism. With this essay, I began to emphasis the conjunction in the phrase "Essays on the Declaration *and* Us." Subsequent essays would increasingly pay attention, and respond directly, to contemporary events.

GOD IN THE DECLARATION (2019)

The recent Sohrab Ahmari-David French exchange reignited a discussion that erupted earlier in conservative circles, stirred by Patrick Deneen's book about the tremendous successes, and worse failures, of liberalism.[11] (For Deneen, the two are often the same, or two sides of the same coin.) The Ahmari-French exchange added an important dimension to the debate, however, by explicitly involving the religious faiths of the two participants. French is an

11 *Why Liberalism Failed* (Yale University Pres, 2018).

Evangelical Christian, Ahmari, a fairly recent convert to Roman Catholicism. With them, Christianity entered into the discussion over how conservatives should view liberalism.

As part of his response to Ahmari, French tweeted the famous lines from the Declaration of Independence concerning all men being created equal and those that immediately follow on the origins of free government, then he asked if Ahmari and his ilk would, or could, subscribe to them?[12] The Declaration was thus presented as a touchstone of American creed and commitment. Shortly before the nation's Fourth of July anniversary, therefore, our attention was led back to this founding document, this "expression of the American mind," this time with specific, and large, questions in mind. How *is* the Declaration with respect to God? How should Christians stand vis-à-vis its presentation of the divine?

God in the Text

To begin with the obvious: God is present in the Declaration. He is mentioned or referred to four times. He is presented as Creator, Legislator, Provident, and Supreme Judge. Men are created equal, Nature is lawful, and both are connected with God and his

---

12   The passage he tweeted: "We hold these truths to be self-evident, that all men are created equal, that they are endowed by their Creator with certain unalienable Rights, that among these are Life, Liberty and the pursuit of Happiness.—That to secure these rights, Governments are instituted among Men, deriving their just powers from the consent of the governed,—That whenever any Form of Government becomes destructive of these ends, it is the Right of the People to alter or to abolish it, and to institute new Government, laying its foundation on such principles and organizing its powers in such form, as to them shall seem most likely to effect their Safety and Happiness. Prudence, indeed, will...."

activity—precisely the activities of creating and legislating. These two features occur at the beginning of the document. The other two show up near the end. As scholarship has shown, the last two references were added to Jefferson's draft by the Continental Congress. They have the effect of "beefing up" the portrait of the divine. Providence is protective and can be relied upon; the Supreme Judge scrutinizes human activity "the world" over and penetrates to the "intentions" of agents. Considered together, human beings can take heart in the thought of superordinate protection as they engage in rightful action, while also knowing that they and it are subject to the most discerning Gaze.

A Divine Political Animal?

The scholar Gregg Frazer has called this theological package "theistic rationalism."[13] Theistic rationalism is halfway between the clockwork god of deism and the Christian orthodoxy of the day; its lodestar is Reason, not Scripture, creed, or tradition. It is a rationalistic religious faith tailored to classical liberal politics, one held by a number of Founders. So argues Professor Frazer.

There is a good deal in the document to support this characterization. The Declaration's Deity is, if you'll pardon the phrase, very much a political animal. His concern, his norms, bear upon men in political community, not in ecclesial communion.[14]

---

13 *The Religious Beliefs of America's Founders: Reason, Revelation, and Revolution* (University of Kansas Press, 2012).
14 The Preamble's Deity, the supreme Legislator, has established "Laws of Nature" that establish "powers," that is "separate and equal" "people[s]": "When in the Course of human events, it becomes necessary for one people to dissolve the political bands which have connected them with another, and to assume among the powers of the earth, the separate and equal station to which the Laws of Nature and of Nature's God entitle them."

Moreover, it is not just any sort of political community he favors, but one that publicly recognizes the Creator's equal endowment of inalienable rights and is properly established to protect them.

A political animal, the Declaration's God also favors human liberty. He has created his human creature free and independent, for political and civil freedom. This helps account for the paradox that the signers of the Declaration expressly rely on Providence *and* that the Declaration is a call to strenuous human action, revolutionary action in fact. The reconciliation is found in the fact that revolution is for freedom and independence, the known will of the Creator. God-given and God-willed, freedom must be humanly exercised, defended, and established.

Of course, as we saw in the previous chapter, this is freedom subject to, and to be guided by, objective moral norms, from natural rights to moral virtues.[15] Moreover, gratitude to, as well as acknowledged reliance on, the Creator should also characterize what we could call "Declaration freedom."

More Political Dimensions

Others have noted the political character of the Deity in the Declaration as well. Some time ago, George Anastaplo argued that the Declaration's God is a political model, crafted for two purposes. First, to show what human political leadership should aspire to, whether it be in legislating, executing, or judging; second, to show that because the unity of legislative, executive, and judicial power in the Deity coexists with omniscience and impeccable rectitude, fallible human beings rightly divide political power and do not

15　As we also noted in the previous chapter, when it comes to warfare, it must observe the distinction between civilized and barbarous or savage conduct, itself a matter of making and respecting appropriate distinctions.

give all political authority into one set of hands.[16] One might call this the Declaration version of "man, the (imperfect) image of God."

Other scholars have emphasized the political character of the document in yet another sense. By this they mean its character as a deliberate compromise, perhaps even obfuscating differences for the sake of presenting a common front for practical purposes. Theistic rationalism's straddling of the differences between deism and orthodoxy would fit this description. In a similar vein, Wilson Carey McWilliams noted the occurrence of Reformed Christianity vocabulary in what he believed to be an otherwise largely Lockean text, instancing the important term "institute," which allowed Calvinists to see something of themselves in the theory of government proclaimed by the Declaration.[17] At the very least, this claim has the virtue of reminding us of the highly communal understanding of human liberty that informed many Americans of the time, about which Barry Shain has written extensively.[18]

Peter Lawler focused on the Congressional additions of "Providence" and "Supreme Judge" in making the case that the Declaration was a statesmanlike compromise between Jefferson's purer Lockean draft and the more orthodox believers among the Founders and the populace. However, when Lawler wrote on Orestes Brownson, he followed Brownson's lead in making the Declaration a thoroughly Lockean document, which, purportedly, enshrined "political atheism." Instead of a tension, there was a one-sided resolution. The estimable scholar of Locke and of the founding, Michael Zuckert,

16 Hence the definition of tyranny as "all power in one set of hands" well-known to Montesquieu and the Founders.
17 "Governments are instituted among men, ... it is the right of the People to institute new Government...."
18 *The Myth of American Individualism* (Princeton University Press, 1996). A more succinct presentation can be found in *Vital Remnants: America's Founding and the Western Tradition* (ISI Books, 2006).

has done the same.[19] However, the "statesmanlike compromise" position seems to me to be more exegetically and historically correct.

A Common Authority

Given all this, what light does our survey shed on the controversy with which we started? It shows that David French was precipitous in the use he made of the passage from the Declaration that evoked the Creator. He presented it as a norm that a Christian can and should accept, apparently without much further ado. However, the fuller argument from which it is taken, and the fuller portrait of the Deity in the document, should give an orthodox Christian believer at least some pause, precisely because the Deity is so politically—and this-worldly—focused. In the Declaration, the "course of human events" that takes place under Providence leads to the first rightly established polity, not to the spread of the Word, much less a Second Coming and Last Judgment. In other words, the theology limned in the Declaration is more accurately styled a political theology, what one could call in hindsight, fledgling America's "civil religion."

As such, it arguably served its purpose at the time and for a long time. But given that from the point of view of consistent liberal thought, its theological components seem to be extraneous additions and, from the point of view of Christian orthodoxy, that it has severe theological deficiencies, one cannot be too surprised that, eventually, each would want to strike out on its own. This certainly seems to be the case with progressive liberalism today. It

19 Michael Zuckert, *The Natural Rights Republic: Studies in the Foundation of the American Political Tradition* (University of Notre Dame Press, 1997). Zuckert has also proposed an "amalgam" thesis concerning the American founding. In it, Lockean elements were central and fundamental to the political philosophy of the Founders, but other pre-modern and biblical elements found a place.

would be understandable for Christian theology to reciprocate. Unlike progressive liberalism, however, which constantly looks forward, Christian theology, to be faithful to its nature, needs to look back to its roots, to its sources and authorities.

Augustine and Us

One authority that the Evangelical French and the Catholic Ahmari might agree on is Augustine. His monumental *City of God* seems remarkably relevant to this Fourth of July dispute, with its critique of civil theology and human hubris and its account of two cities and how they are inextricably mixed in this life as they proceed to eternity. One thing the late Peter Augustine Lawler used to emphasize in this connection is that after Augustine the human person could not be totally claimed by the state and the state could not rightly claim to possess or dictate religious truth. That would be a most important lesson for all Christians—indeed all Americans—to relearn this day. Paradoxically, it would have the additional benefit of reminding us that religious liberty, both individual and corporate, and its correlative, the limited state, are important common ground shared by classical Christianity and what we could call the Declaration's "Christianity-adjacent" theistic liberalism.

CHAPTER FIVE

As the same time as I began my career as an essayist on "the Declaration and Us," I began an adjunct career as a critic of tendentious or misleading readings of the Declaration. A few months after my inaugural essay, I penned a critical review of a winsome effort by a rather famous academic to coopt the Declaration for contemporary progressive ends. While admiring the author's passion and charm, I could not let that misguided endeavor go unchallenged.

The famous academic was Danielle Allen, daughter of the well-known conservative political scientist, William B. Allen; the book was *Our Declaration: A Reading of the Declaration of Independence in Defense of Equality*. The title of the review came from John Austin's famous book, appealed to by Ms. Allen in hers. My use, however, was ironic.

HOW TO DO THINGS WITH WORDS (2014)

This is an impassioned book about the Declaration of Independence. It comes from specific personal and pedagogical experiences, as its author, Danielle Allen, a classicist and political theorist at Princeton, winsomely reports.

Ms. Allen employs several techniques, some old, some new, in engaging and pursuing her book's central object: what she calls a close, "sentence by sentence," reading of the document, one that sometimes lingers over the meaning of a single term but that also draws upon modern theories of the uses to which language can be put. But while the methods are specific, the aim is quite grand and ambitious: to make the Declaration "our Declaration," with "us" being not just all Americans, of whatever race or socioeconomic condition, but all humanity.

As one can see, the Declaration has stirred Allen mightily. She describes teaching it as a transformative experience, and she has responded to it with all of her being, as a scholar, a citizen, and a human being. This is "engaged scholarship" in a fulsome sense.

Our Declaration: A Reading of the Declaration of Independence in Defense of Equality is also clearly conceived and written. Auto-biographical revelations of her as a young girl growing up in a re-markably bookish and talkative family, and the young teacher's recounting of a decade of teaching the Declaration to advantaged and disadvantaged students at the University of Chicago, lay the foundation for the close reading that follows. Seeking to lay bare the "philosophical argument" of the text, she sees the Declaration as a specimen of "political philosophy" that should be read as such.

In keeping with that classical category, she also sees it as a "prac-tical syllogism," with "principles" and "facts" brought together to conclude with a "judgment." The facts indicate that King George is a tyrant, and the facts, together with the principles of free govern-ment, indicate the moral-political "necessity" of avoiding encroach-ing despotism by declaring independence. Inspired by such writers as the British philosopher J. L. Austin (*How to Do Things with Words*, 1962), she further sees the Declaration as a series of community-forming and community-performed "actions" on the part of the signers and other colonists. It is also a community-dissolving action, of course, and Allen works the "divorce" (with Great Britain) and "marriage" (of the states with one another) metaphors rather hard.

Reading Behind the Text

But because she believes that even close textual analysis does not account for everything of importance conveyed in the text, she also gives a focused account of the prehistory of its composition, in which "politicos" John Adams and Richard Henry Lee, the Continental Congress and its numerous committees, Thomas Jefferson, of course, and even calligraphers and printers, play important roles. This history is important to her because she wishes to make a central point about the character of democratic thinking and action: it involves a wide array of minds, it's messy, it occasions large amounts of formal and informal talk, and while it works toward unanimity, whatever is achieved becomes the predicate for more talk.

The two biggest issues surfaced by the contextual reading are the excision of Jefferson's diatribe against slavery and the slave trade from his original draft (as insisted upon by the delegates from South Carolina and Georgia), and the addition by the Congress itself of two designations of the Deity ("Supreme Judge of the World" and "Divine Providence) that go beyond Jefferson's "Nature's God." (Earlier, the drafting committee had added "Creator" to Jefferson's handiwork.) The deletion sadly indicates the downsides of democratic writing and decision-making, where the necessity to win votes sometimes wins out over the truth. The additions seem to be a little more confounding for Allen—she is unsure, in the end, what to make of God and religious affirmations in the Declaration.

Like many today, she wants her egalitarianism to rest on a secular foundation. This, one suspects, is the deeper meaning of her oft-used term, "commitment," which is what human beings do when they cannot affirm a principle on the basis of either faith or reason. Certainly, the naturalistic egalitarian anthropology she teases out of the text is more sketched than demonstrated and with significant lacunae. For a better treatment of the character of the Deity affirmed in the Declaration, one could begin by consulting Gregg L. Frazer's *The Religious Beliefs of America's Founders* (2012) and his useful concept of "theistic rationalism," halfway between

Deism and eighteenth-century Christian orthodoxy. That would be a good start. Allen actually gets close to Frazer's view, but her manner of reading finally precludes her from considering in a comprehensive way the Declaration's teaching about the Deity.

Interpretive Lacunae

In fact, Allen's hermeneutics tend to be somewhat piecemeal. At the first occurrence of an important term, she pauses and tries to wring meaning from it, often employing etymology and analogy. However, she hardly ever takes two equally necessary measures: bringing together the various occurrences of the term so as to think about them as a conceptual whole, and looking up the term's range of meanings in the eighteenth century.

A key instance of this is her treatment of "State." She ignores the important features of statehood listed in the final paragraph of the document ("as Free and Independent States, they have full Power to ...."). A related instance is the Preamble's phrase "laws of Nature," which James Stoner has rightly connected with a proto-version of international law, as well as the natural rights philosophy of John Locke.[20] Allen displays her characteristic ingenuity in coming to terms with the words "State" and "the laws of Nature," but her constructions—the State as a people organized with the institutions and capacity for collective activity, the laws of nature as one people's recognition of another's natural desire to survive, as a necessary condition of being recognized in turn—ignore text and history.

In general, with these lacunae her readings regularly risk displaying the exegete's creativity more than the patent or plausible meanings of the words on the page. Her analysis is uneasily poised between seeking to be faithful to the original meaning of the text,

20 http://www.nlnrac.org/american/declaration-of-independence.

exploring the meanings she claims to find, and advancing the contemporary political and cultural ideas to which she subscribes.

One telling instance of the latter is her refusal to say "husband" and "wife" in connection with marriage; she persistently writes "spouses" or "partners." The capacious egalitarianism that she finds in the text comports with—or is made to comport with— contemporary progressive commitments. This is eisegesis, rather than exegesis, the cardinal sin of the exegete.

Equality

Allen writes, as she says in her title, "in defense of equality," and this means reviving our "egalitarian commitment" as a democratic people. "If we abandon equality," she says, "we lose *the single bond* that makes us a community, that makes us a people with the capacity to be free collectively and individually in the first place" (emphasis added). On the important question of the relationship between freedom and equality, her view is that "If the Declaration can stake a claim to freedom, it is *only because* it is so clear-eyed about the fact that the people's strength resides in its equality" (emphasis added).

This, assuredly, is a heavy burden to place upon equality. It comes as no surprise, then, that her understanding of it is quite substantial and rather complex. For example, while she regularly defines equality as "political equality," she includes under this rubric widespread "economic opportunity" and the ability to "understand when excessive material inequality undermines broad democratic participation." Similarly, political equality requires, if not equal educational attainment, the considerable goal of "the empowerment of human beings as language-using creatures"—that is, "the capacity of citizens to use language effectively enough to influence the choices we make together."

This expansive umbrella of meanings of "political equality" (and I have only given a partial list) fits with her characterization of equality as an "idea" and an "ideal" that have never been realized on this earth. The mere fact that a people has embraced this idea would seem to be a cause of wonder, but she takes it for granted. For his part, Tocqueville knew that Americans' unusual idealism, born of a melding of Protestantism and Enlightenment rationalism, was cause for wonder, and he saw the need to trace its historical genealogy. Moreover, he warned that democratic idealism, a human world wholly captive to a vision of equality and popular sovereignty, needed to be carefully monitored for its excesses, lest new forms of despotism arise.[21] True lovers of democracy needed to learn to love it well, that is, moderately, as Pierre Manent put it at the end of his book on *Tocqueville and the Nature of Democracy*.[22]

As for herself, Allen confesses to her "own driven commitment to egalitarian democracy." Allen's passions and worries are not Tocqueville's. Her dire assessment of the declining fortunes of this idea among politicians, parties, and the populace leads her to express perhaps her greatest fear: "I for one cannot bear to see the ideal of equality pass away before it has reached its full maturity." To which she adds a poignant *cri de coeur*: "I hope I am not alone."

While several discrete discussions spell them out, one passage aims to summarize the complex of meanings she finds in, or ascribes to, the concept of equality in the text of the Declaration:

> There are five facets of the ideal of equality for which
> the Declaration argues. The first facet . . . describes the
> kind of equality that exists when neither of two parties
> can dominate the other. The second facet concerns the

---

21 Volume 1 of *Democracy in America* explored "the tyranny of the majority," while Volume 2 limned the prospect of a despotic tutelary state.

22 Pierre Manent, *Tocqueville and the Nature of Democracy* (Rowman & Littlefield, 1996), p. 132.

importance to humankind of having equal access to the
tool of government, the most important instrument
each of us has for securing the future.... The third facet
concerns the value of egalitarian approaches to the development of collective intelligence.... The fourth facet
concerns egalitarian practices of reciprocity.... And the
fifth facet has to do with the equality entailed in sharing ownership of public life and in co-creating our
common world.

The paraphrasal language is striking coming from someone
who claims to be engaged in a close reading, and it is hard to think
we are in Jefferson's or eighteenth-century Americans' thought
world. Clearly this method of reading has more to it than "close"
and "sentence by sentence" commitments, or even single-word
focus. Often there are "assumptions" and "implications" and "performative meanings" to unpack, and "images" and "metaphors" to
interpret. As already noted, the twin dangers in this are 1) over-
looking what's really contained in terms and sentences in accor-
dance with plausible original meanings, and 2) importing her own
by eisegesis.

One Nation or One People?

Some of these importations she is aware of. Let us take as an example the word "nation." Early on she employs it in speaking of
the entity that resulted from the Declaration of Independence.
She wants Declaration-America to be both a federation of states
and a nation (if only incipiently). Finally, though, she has to acknowledge that Declaration-America was not a nation but, according to the terminology of the text, a "people": "although their
new confederation is not yet a single nation, they have become
one people."

This issue is important for many reasons, all bearing upon the proper understanding of the complex whole envisaged and achieved by the Declaration. Allen notes, but does not develop, the fact that the Continental Congress established, along with the drafting committee for the Declaration, another committee to write articles of confederation. Three men served on both. The congressionally approved Articles of Confederation were submitted to the states for ratification in late 1777 after a year of debate, and clearly established state sovereignty.[23]

I draw the inference from this that the fledgling Americans were still rather unclear about what flowed from their political principles, and what the union they were forming truly was and entailed. The need for a better understanding of federalism, of *e pluribus unum*, would make itself felt in the subsequent decade-plus, leading to the Constitutional Convention and to the last-minute (serendipitous or providential) inclusion by Gouverneur Morris of the phrase "We the People of the United States" in the Preamble, which tipped the scales from sovereign states to a sovereign People that could consider itself a nation.

However, it took much subsequent history, including a Civil War and three amendments to the Constitution, to confirm and codify that reality (and even then it was far from realized). Allen's declaredly ahistorical reading of the Declaration (which she departs from when it suits her purpose), and her present-day political commitments, don't allow her to enter adequately into "the American mind" on display in the text.

"Democracy"

In this connection, the most telling piece of eisegesis is the author's central term, "democracy"—a word not found in the Declaration

23 https://avalon.law.yale.edu/18th_century/artconf.asp.

of Independence. Nor is this an innocent substitution or importation. Allen is not wholly unaware of the fact that the Founders, vigorously debating political regimes and forms, by and large used "democracy" as a term of opprobrium. It was contrasted with "republic"; and even the latter term does not capture the normative thinking about political principles and forms of those who deliberated on these matters at the time. As the political philosopher James W. Ceaser has rightly argued (*Liberal Democracy and Political Science*, 1990), the American regime is a "hybrid," and its proper nomenclature must perforce be compound: liberal democracy; constitutional republic; or partly-federal, partly-national in character. Allen's imported term "democracy" already foreshortens her thinking, as well as tipping the balance in a certain partisan direction. Already indicated by her privileging and enhancing of equality, the importing of "democracy" into her reading of the Declaration clearly bespeaks partisan hands at work on the document. In so doing, she anticipates what will become the partisan use and indeed fetishism of the term by progressives and the Democratic Party. Later in our essays, starting with Chapter Eight, with the help of the French political philosopher Pierre Manent, we will consider the "effectual truth" of this reworking of the notion of "democracy."

A Brief Conclusion

My two main objections to this in many ways impressive interpretive effort are therefore clear. The author's hermeneutics are not adequate to their object and her political commitments predispose her to see things that are not in the text or miss those that are. Still, it is important, I believe, to note this evidence of the enduring appeal and normative power that emanate from the document that has been called (by Pauline Maier) "America's Scripture." Even those who depart significantly from its teaching want to enlist its authority.

It remains to better scholarship—informed by historical, philosophical, and exegetical learning—to bring this text's original and enduring meaning to light for all citizens to consider. They should read Danielle Allen's egalitarian effort, but others as well, perhaps starting with Michael Zuckert's "structural" reading in *The Natural Rights Republic* (1999). However, since both Allen and Zuckert suffer from a shyness about the issue of the Deity in the Declaration, it is important not to leave out Gregg Frazer's work referenced above. Or reread Chapter Four above.[24]

---

24 From what we could call the older literature on the Declaration, I would single out Paul Eidelberg's *On the Silence of the Declaration of Independence* (University of Massachusetts Press, 1976) for special commendation.

Chapter Six

In the period in which these essays appeared there is a clear division: Before Trump and After Trump (and "division" in more than one sense). With the advent of Donald Trump, first as a candidate, then as President, always as a partisan pugilist, a figure appeared on the political scene that could not be ignored. As a secular "sign of contradiction," along with him came numerous revelations, revelations about the state of the Republican Party, revelations about the nature of the Democratic Party, and of contemporary Progressivism more broadly. In the literal sense of the term, he inaugurated an "apocalyptic" time, a time of clarifying unveiling.

Simultaneously, it was a time of the partisan hysteria that Montesquieu said was characteristic of a free society. In the maelstrom of charges and countercharges, it was difficult to get one's bearings, difficult to grasp and assess reality. The next essay attempted to make a contribution to that difficult task in mid-2016. It asked, what does the Declaration tell us about the despot and despotism, the charge that both candidates and parties were levelling at the other party's standard-bearer? Given that the Declaration is the patrimony of all Americans, it was offered to partisans and independents alike. So as not to prejudice the conclusion, I stayed at a very general level.

DARK TIMES, THE DECLARATION, AND THE DESPOTIC EXECUTIVE (2016)

It's been a year since my last little piece on the Declaration of Independence and what a year it's been!

45

On the Right of our political spectrum, one could sum up its events and eventfulness in one word: Trump. A party has been captured by an outsider, the disaffection of millions of its rank-and-file revealed. At the national level, the Grand Old Party is not so grand or even particularly coherent, and some fear it might not last as a party. Something similar can be said of the party of the Left. Substitute "Clinton" and "Sanders" and comparable deep fissures emerge, although perhaps with less likelihood of disintegration. The energy, however, clearly rests with the insurgents against the Establishment.

What light, in terms of principles and manner of thinking about politics, might the Declaration shed on this confusing situation?

To begin with, it cannot give us direct insights into parties and their role in our liberal democratic order. As Stephen Skowronek noted a while back, the Declaration was penned in a much different context: at the beginning of a period of "patrician politics" in which parties were deemed equivalent to factions, dead set against the common good.[25] Harvey C. Mansfield Jr.'s classic study, *Statesmanship and Party Government*,[26] deftly analyzed the arguments that led to their acceptance in Great Britain, while any number of fine studies of American political development have detailed their roots in, and rise in the aftermath of, the Washington administration.[27] The Declaration is silent on or ignorant of all that.

25   Stephen Skowronek, *The Politics Presidents Make* (Harvard University Press, 1993).

26   Harvey C. Mansfield, Jr., *Statesmanship and Party Government* (University of Chicago Press, 1965).

27   I would recommend *The American Constitution: Its Origins and Development* (W. W. Norton and Co., 1991 (7th edition)), by Alfred H. Kelly, Winfred A. Harbison, and Herman Belz. I am also partial to Harry V. Jaffa's "The Nature and Origin of the American Party System," in *Political Parties USA*, edited by Robert A. Goldwin (Rand McNally, 1964).

However, one can turn the question around and ask, what did, or more to the point, what do the parties think about the Declaration? Today, many progressive liberals and Democrats have an incoherent view of the Declaration, but one that jibes with their worldview and serves progressive purposes. On the one hand, they insist that the Declaration was penned by misogynist, slave-holding, privileged white males; on the other, it is the American charter of egalitarian freedom, setting forth "ideals" and "aspirations" that History will make good. Partisans on the Right tend to have a more positive view, sometimes speaking of the Founders' wisdom, other times using it as a marker to indicate "just how far we've departed." And its revolutionary spirit continues to resonate with many who suffer or perceive the menacing hand of arbitrary government.

Today's Partisan Alarums

It is in this context that we can turn to today's chaotic partisan situation. Quite noticeably, both parties loathe and fear the other party's standard-bearer and angrily denounce him or her with jarring epithets, of which "crook" and "liar" are two of the mildest, escalating to "authoritarian," "fascist," and "dictator." In this heated situation, the Declaration's description of the moral character and nefarious deeds of George III takes on a surprising relevance and can serve a contemporary purpose as a portrait of a despot and a checklist for assessment of the validity of partisan charges and characterizations. In what follows, therefore, I will sketch in the broadest terms the Declaration's checklist, leaving it to the reader to fill it in and apply it. In so doing, I am not denying that I have my own partisan feelings and judgments. Here, however, I wish to emulate the Declaration's own appeal to principle and reason in politically stressful times.

A Tripartite Scheme

To begin with, we can note that the Declaration took seriously the reality of the tyrant or despot, therefore so can we—but guided, as it was, by articulable principles and a concern for "Facts" (a term that has acquired great salience these days). The Declaration points toward a tripartite analysis of the tyrant and of tyranny: 1) the agent's moral character; 2) his or her aims or "design," whether declared or inferred from acts; and 3) his or her "troops" or accomplices, legislative and other. Following this template can help change partisan epithets to (at least plausible) understanding. To be sure, doing so will entail a good deal of critical sifting of information. One may have to be satisfied with what used to be called "moral certainty." Such is the nature of the political beast.

The Executive, or Tyrant, vis-à-vis the Other Branches of Government

Secondly, all of this is to be situated and judged within a normative framework of rightly constituted government, with "guards" of the sovereign People's "security," "liberty," and "the public good" at the helm. In the case before us, with a special focus on the responsibilities of the executive. Primary among these is the view of "legislative bodies," "legislation," and "law" held by the prospective chief executive. Why primary? Because the legislative is the first of the "just powers" of government and law or legislation is the first topic in the list of usurpations and injuries by the Crown with which the Declaration deals. Of the twenty-seven listed, it occupies the first seven, with two more later in the list. This should not surprise. What is to be "executed" by the chief *executive*, if not the laws?[28] From there, one should trace what the

28   To this focus on the executive's relationship to legislative bodies, leg-

Declaration has to say about its relationship to the judiciary and to the military.[29] All of this can and should factor into one's assessment of today's candidates for chief executive officer of the country.

Readying for Action

Lastly, the Declaration indicates that political analysis and thinking are tied to action, perhaps even bold action. As such, it necessarily involves risk-taking and hope. The Declaration exhibits its own grounds for hope in its conviction of the rightness of its cause, the regard of the Deity, and the resolve and collaboration of like-minded lovers of liberty. While not dispositive (material force needs to be considered), these should all be factors in a political calculation.

In the Declaration, therefore, we have a double mirror, one side in which to consider the two candidates, the other side, ourselves. For we too have to ask, what are we citizens to do, given our analysis and assessment of the two candidates and of the political situation more generally? The Declaration makes clear that even revolutionary action *can* be warranted. But it also lays down strict criteria for such action. It thus cautions boldness to tether itself to principled, prudential reason, while challenging reason to entertain thoughts of both the worst and the boldest. Possible despotism is perhaps the greatest challenge for political reason. The Declaration wants us to get it right.[30]

islation, and what we could call "positive law," one should add a concern for his relationship to two types of fundamental law limned in the document: the "constitution" and "the laws of Nature."

29 We treat these relations in our last chapter, "Government Under Judgment."

30 One does not need a crystal ball to suggest that the reader should keep this chapter handy in order to navigate the (utterly predictable) partisan recriminations in the 2024 election cycle.

Chapter Seven

In a similar non-partisan vein, I penned the following essay. In it, I tried to construct a dialogue between partisans of identity politics and the Declaration. Aristotle said that one of the most important works of the political philosopher is to mediate between partisan claims of justice. I tried to follow his example. Truth be told, however, I did so, in the biblical phrase, "hoping against hope."

THE DECLARATION
AND IDENTITY POLITICS (2018)

Two recent Law and Liberty essays addressed identity politics in our day. Neither article spoke in its favor. One argued that the demand for recognition of all identities was impracticable, therefore undesirable.[31] The other used identity politics as a template for critiquing Justice Kennedy's majority decision in *Masterpiece Cakeshop*.[32] Together, they pointed to the increased salience of identity claims in our culture and politics. Of course, these commentators are not the first to note this fact. Rod Dreher, for example, has argued for some time now that the Left's identity politics necessarily will, and in fact has, engendered a Right-response, including, but

---

31 https://lawliberty.org/the-politics-of-identity-is-undone-by-the-impracticality-of-achieving-recognition/.
32 https://lawliberty.org/masterpiece-cakeshop-and-the-crisis-of-identity-politics/.

not limited to, the alt-Right.[33] You reap what you sow, especially if you sow dragon's teeth.

On this Fourth of July, I thought I would bring the Declaration into dialogue with identity politics. Admittedly, there is a problem at the outset with dialogue between the parties.

A Serious American Mind

Proponents of identity politics most often ignore the Declaration. When they do speak of it, two apparently conflicting attitudes inform what they say. The stirring claim that "all men are created equal" is said to be a sham statement, in reality restricted to white males, while, in the next breath, the document is said to limn positive "ideals" that History will fill in, in an ever-more egalitarian, emancipatory, and inclusive way. Neither way takes the text seriously.

The Declaration, however, is nothing if not serious. Serious about politics. Serious about human action. Serious about thinking well and about truth ("we hold these truths"; "let facts be submitted to a candid world"). Serious too about change, including revolutionary change. Serious therefore about community and its right order. Serious about making itself intelligible and persuasive to relevant audiences (while also discriminating between good and bad audiences).

In all these ways, its seriousness entails the sovereignty of reason in the soul and requires the rational control of sentiment or passion, especially the political passions: love of liberty and love of justice, indignation before injustice and fear before encroaching despotism. In its seriousness, therefore, the Declaration can serve

---

33 For examples, see Dreher's "The Perils of Identity Politics" (November 9, 2016), "The Curse of Identity Politics" (August 13, 2017), and "Identity Politics Ruin Everything" (December 12, 2017).

as a template for, or, as need be, comment on, the various proponents of identity politics.

Seriousness Versus Indignation

The Declaration's seriousness about justice and injustice is an important initial point of contact with identity politics and its proponents. Certainly, the latter come to sight as very much moved by a passion for justice, or more precisely, by resentment at injustice. How so? They are indignant denouncers, often of a vociferous sort.

Now, anger is, if not *the*, certainly a central political passion. Not by chance was it the first passion Aristotle treated in the *Rhetoric*. On the other hand, his analysis of partisan claims of justice in the *Politics* showed that each, at best, has a partial grasp of the truth, but mistakenly takes its view as the whole. It was the special task of "political philosophy" to display, then reconcile, these shortcomings, just as it was the rhetorician's task to curb and channel indignation with his speech.

It is instructive, therefore, to contrast the Declaration's seriousness of reasoning and purpose, its control of passion at the service of serious action, with the passionate indignation typical of many proponents of identity politics. In this connection, one could ask Bret Weinstein (formerly) of Evergreen University or the Christakises of Yale University about the open-minded, dialogic, character of the proponents they encountered. It was conspicuous by its absence, indeed conspicuous as its antithesis.

Perhaps a step up would be to consider and compare texts, for example, of the Platform of the Movement for Black Lives with the Declaration. However, here too one finds aggressive assertions followed by six groups of "Demands" that, taken together, indict (almost) all of America and American history and call for a total remaking of the country. America's founding "revolution of sober expectations"[34] (Martin Diamond), aiming to establish "new guards" for its security, contrasts rather starkly with a text that envisages "a complete transformation of the current systems."[35]

Many other instances could be adduced, but it is undeniable that indignation and indictment, deep indignation and wide-spread indictment, play an important role in identity politics. Confronting this fact, a dispassionate observer could be forgiven for recalling the adage that passion is a bad counselor, and the same observer could with reason ask, what is the idea of justice, what are the facts of injustice, driving and fueling the passion? There is still a need "to give an account" of one's views, no matter how passionately held. Facts must be adduced and ascertained, principles articulated and defended, if such charges and claims are to receive reason's imprimatur.

In connection with recent powder-keg moments for identity politics, there are the awkward facts that George Zimmerman was acquitted by a jury of his peers and the FBI under Eric Holder exonerated Darren Wilson, the policeman who struggled with, shot, and killed Michael Brown in Ferguson, MO. "Hands up! Don't shoot!" turned out to be unverified and most unlikely. The turn to "symbolic truth" afterwards was an acknowledgement of misjudgment on the plane of the particular and a *petitio principii* on the more general plane of principle.

Justice Against Justice?

The demands of identity politics, of course, do not always come in such direct and vociferous forms. In academe, for instance, we

34 https://www.aei.org/research-products/book/the-revolution-of-sober-expectations/.

35 These "systems" include "the patriarchal family," i. e., the monogamous heterosexual couple and coupling in view of the natural procreating and rearing of children. This is a staple of radical thought since at least Engels.

encounter them not just in shouting students, but in professors and Dean's offices posting notices about microaggressions. Certain talismans such as "diversity" (along with "equity" and "inclusion") go through all levels of the institution. Harvard University, a bell-wether in these areas,[36] has shown the two sides of this ideal and criterion, with separate ceremonies to celebrate the achievements of certain identities and, more darkly, denigrating the "personality traits," i.e., character, of other racial and ethnic groups when it comes to the all-important gatekeeping function of admissions.[37] Thus, identity politics can range from the hot to the cool, from the overt to the backroom fix. In the name of a higher justice, it can violate ordinary justice.

The last claim is the nub. Deliberately ambiguous on my part, the sentence could be the protest of common moral sense against invidious discrimination, against violations of a fundamental prin-ciple of justice: treating equals equally and unequals unequally. On this reading, the Declaration's individualistic notion of justice would comport with common sense and would be an enlargement and a specification, precisely a *political* specification and enlarge-ment, of its core intuitions. In *this* political community, it is indi-viduals who have rights, not groups; the decisive group is the

---

36 https://lawliberty.org/discrimination-against-asian-americans-re-veals-the-ugliness-of-racial-selection-harvard-lawsuit-drew-gilpin-faust/

37 The reality of these invidious practices was confirmed, and Harvard was found constitutionally in error, in *Students for Fair Admission v. Harvard* (2023). More recently, the obscenely equivocating testi-mony of three high-profile university presidents before Congress and the demonstrated plagiarism of the then Harvard president, Clau-dine Gay, have brought the noxious character of the DEI regime in American higher education to increased public awareness. For a fine analysis of its nature and immorality, see Bishop Robert Barron: https://www.wordonfire.org/articles/barron/ivy-league/.

community of individuals who come together in social compact to defend its members' rights, as well as to exercise the right of self-government for the sake of the "Safety and Happiness" of the community. Injustices and adjustments there will and must be, but they should be judged and addressed from within this framework. Sometimes, it is sadly true, they will involve bloody Civil War.

On the other hand, the sentence could speak for identity politics, which believes that, due to past injustices, all identities are not currently equal, so rectificatory justice calls for the suspension of other forms of justice. When it has done its work, then the other sorts can resume their place and work. This was Justice Sandra Day O'Connor's view. It is New York City mayor Bill de Blasio's view.

Abstract Individuals Versus Concrete Identities

In this way, certain contrasts come to sight. The Declaration's notion of justice focused, fundamentally, on individuals and their rights, while race, sex, and gender were largely abstracted from.[38] Identity politics finds this abstraction a hypocritical sham and a cover for injustice, starting with the black slaves denied their unalienable rights. Justice *is* human equality, identity politics agrees, but equality must be real, not merely legal or formal, and it must be across-the-board, for all identities. In the all-important area of race, the movement has been from affirmative action to quotas to proportional representation.

Identity politics is thus a continuation of a tradition of critique of the abstractness, the "mere" formality and "hypocrisy" of the classical liberal notion of justice. Anatole France gave it classic formulation: "Rich and poor are equally forbidden to sleep under

38 I say "largely" because of the Declaration's recognition of the need, in justice, for differential treatment of age, sex, and condition in the conduct of civilized warfare.

bridges." In this view, what are called "formal freedoms" are really masks of oppression and means of manipulation, both of minds ("false consciousness") and bodies. Likewise, equality under the law, its equal protection for all, masks and perpetuates past and ongoing inequities.

What identity politics adds to this familiar litany is two-fold. It adds to the list of the oppressed, expanding from race, class, and sex (women) to sex (homosexuals) and gender (transgendered), with the categories being constantly tweaked (LGBTQIA+), precisely in response to the demands of identity. It also adds a new sovereign category and focus of justice: the group, rather than discrete individuals.

"Blacks" become as important in this optic as Martin Luther King, Jr. and Frederick Douglass, who are extolled (when they are extolled) primarily for their service to the group. The individual thus risks being defined primarily as a member and representative of a group. This is almost the reverse of King's dream of a nation in which one's children "will not be judged by the color of their skin but by the content of their character."

As the two eminent (and rather different) examples suggest, this group-identity version of justice is an act of injustice to superior individuals and, *mutatis mutandis*, to all the individuals of the group, who, after all, do have the right to be judged on the content of their character. In a connected vein, when the group is defined in a partial or ideological way, as it most often is,[39] certain members, precisely those with different views of identity or justice, are tacitly excluded, or decried as traitors. It is amazing how many "Uncle Toms" there are in America! One begins to suspect that group identity is too slippery to employ as a, much less *the*, criterion of justice.

39 See Mike Gonzales, *The Plot to Change America* (Encounter Books, 2020). Its first part is entitled "And Activists Created Groups."

Tertium Datur?

A hopeful reconciliation of the two would suggest that each view needs something the other has and both need to give up something of themselves in return. The abstract individual with rights ensures that irrelevant factors—precisely factors such as race, sex, and gender—are not inappropriately brought in to bias judgments of merit. When they are, they can be indicted as such. But no human being is simply an individual; identity matters, and justice sometimes requires factoring in components of identity. While I might score high on a police academy entrance exam, I would be a horrible cop in Baltimore. On the other hand, the abstract individual reminds those who want to make group identity dispositive for justice that it inevitably runs the risk of injustice, including against its own members.

For its part, the Declaration was already aware of the need to complement its abstract individualism with distinguishing content. In view of its revolutionary and political purposes, it identified various *moral* categories that perfect and help define the free individual and "a free People." These included items from the canon of the cardinal virtues, prudence and fortitude, high-toned virtues, magnanimity and manliness, and, in another direction, deference to the Supreme Judge and trust in Divine Providence.

The various identities could likewise adopt them as norms for themselves, precisely as enriching their own identities. In so doing, they would find themselves speaking and acting with the seriousness of the Declaration.

Chapter Eight

Candidate Trump became President Trump and immediately (indeed even before his inauguration) a Resistance formed that declared itself utterly and completely hostile to him and "what he stood for." For reasons understandable and questionable, disproportionate attention was devoted to President Trump, while his virulent opponents were largely given a pass by the media. It became clear whose side the legacy media were on. As a result, it seemed only fair to turn the spotlight on the Resistance and to consider it. Here too Aristotle provided instruction and example. As political animals, the Resistance both speak and act. The first task therefore was to hearken to what they said and did, then from that draw out their views for inspection. As for evaluation, that would take place according to relevant Declaration criteria.

RESISTANCE IN THE LIGHT OF 1776 (2017)

What a year it has been! "Trump wins and the Resistance begins" might sum it up. Into this maelstrom steps our annual "What would the Declaration say?" reflection. We could turn in three directions: toward Trump; toward "the Resistance"; toward the people who fall outside his devoted followers and fierce opponents and who wish to make some contribution to the commonweal in the midst of low-intensity civil war.

In the first case, we would seek for criteria by which to judge his actions (his real, not imagined ones), as well as guidance for him for the future.

In the second, we would look to mine the Declaration for criteria for judging legitimate efforts of resistance and to guide its principled, prudent practice.

Lastly, those who are not in either camp could look to the Declaration to gain perspective on what a steady and calm voice in the melee would sound like.

In our original *Law and Liberty* reflection for the holiday, we noted that the Declaration of Independence bespeaks an American mind that kept its wits in the midst of the storm and stress of dramatically unfolding events. It did so by applying "principles" to "Facts" (that word resonates today), by bringing an entire worldview to bear upon a set of dueling agents and coming to a considered determination to act.

A subsequent essay took its lead from the warnings of the two political camps today concerning the nefarious agenda of the other's standard-bearer. It turned to the Declaration's depiction of the despotic character and deeds of the king of England and tried to draw lessons for analysis and evaluation in contemporary circumstances. Its framework and criteria for assessing an executive remain pertinent.

New since then is that the White House has switched hands—and those opposing the President are now "the Resistance," a group comprising many elements, some well-known, others not. Generalizations are difficult, but that is the nature of the political beast, and they need to be ventured to be confirmed or replaced with better. Since the Resistance does not receive nearly the scrutiny that its target does, it seems fair to turn attention on it for a bit.

Three Objections & An Irony

The Resistance appears to have three fundamental objections to Trump: he does not represent them; he is illegitimate; he is a threat to all they hold dear. The first is a standard democratic (with a small "d") lament after an election, but felt and taken to great lengths. Considered individually, the second and the third are each serious enough to justify resistance, while the three together are compelling, almost overwhelming, stirring deep passions of indignation, frustration, and fear. Add to that contempt for the person and it is a very powerful brew.

Ironically, though, while with their charges the Resistance points to dark clouds on the near horizon, if we look at the charges, we can begin to see other clouds of an equally dark character. Taken together, they suggest a distinctive view of "democracy," one rather exclusive in its inclusivity and monolithic in its view of diversity—in short, arguably as troubling as anything said about its opponent.

A Frenchman Helps Americans

Perhaps surprisingly, the French political philosopher Pierre Manent can orient us in this matter. A few years ago, he observed an emerging "new order" in France (and western Europe more widely):

> The new order now imposing itself more and more on us rests on the contrast between legitimate and illegitimate opinions . . . it already seems clear that with this transformation, we have started to pass from an order built on confrontation of equally legitimate opinions to one built on confrontation between legitimate opinions and illegitimate ones, between political orthodoxy and heresy.[40] He added: "If this were true, then we would be in the process of departing from democracy as we have known it so far."

40 Pierre Manent, "Populist Demagogy and the Fanaticism of the Center," *American Affairs*, Summer 2017.

We Americans can retain three elements from Manent's European observations—a mentality consisting in a starkly binary character ("legitimate" versus "illegitimate" opinions), with a secularly sacred character ("political orthodoxy and heresy"), and a new understanding of "democracy" at work—and look for them in the thought of the Resistance. There are immediate resonances. Trump certainly threatens what it holds dear, what it holds sacred. He, they say, is profane and a profaner. He therefore has to be resisted, this despite having run and won according to the rules of the game.

The Charges in A New Light

Now, Donald Trump in many ways *is* profane. Hillary Clinton's most effective campaign ad brought this obvious truth to our attention. One needs to distinguish, however, his flagrant violations of norms of common morality and decency and his (real or imagined) flouting of Resistance norms and principles. Respect for women, for example, in no way necessarily entails commitment to an absolute abortion license or federal funding for Planned Parenthood. So one can agree with the Resistance in part. But the content of its "sacred," which Trump profanes, remains to be investigated. We will do so in the next chapter with the help of Alexis de Tocqueville and Emile Durkheim.

As for Trump's illegitimacy, in making its accusation, the Resistance straddles two senses of the term—not legitimately elected and morally illegitimate. To bring these senses together, it often employs single words and short phrases—"the popular vote," "Russian interference," "Russia collusion," "misogyny, racism, xenophobia," "deplorables" —so as not to have to distinguish them or expressly defend the imputation. We need not adjudicate the various claims to note that these planks of the anti-Trump platform represent a particular view of the facts in question, each one contestable,[41] and a worldview within which they take on their full significance. It is the latter that is most interesting, because in principle the most determinative.

Some have tried to come to terms with the Resistance's worldview. William Voegeli has done yeoman's work in a number of essays, and we mine his work in the next chapter.[42] The Declaration can make its contribution as well, not by direct comment, of course, but by implied questions and explicit criteria. Here is what it would have us ponder this day.

Declaration Criteria

The Declaration is not averse to worldviews; it has one that it expressed candidly. Has the Resistance expressed its worldview? Candidly? The record is mixed. There is need for further clarification and for openness to criticism and critique. Then there are the three areas referred to above: representation, legitimacy, and existential threat.

The Declaration employs "representation," or rather its cognates, two times. It refers to "Representative Houses" who earlier

---

41 Subsequent revelations showed that the charges involving treason ("Russia collusion") were demonstrably false. Perhaps the greatest "dirty trick" in American political history was the Hillary Clinton campaign-promoted "Steele dossier"-"Russia collusion" hoax aided and abetted by Deep State insiders, Obama administration higher-ups, the Democratic Party, and a compliant mainstream media. The revelation of this conspiracy was among the most important events of the subsequent years, revealing an active collusion against the very foundations of our constitutional and democratic order.

42 William Voegeli, "The New Abnormal," *Claremont Review of Books*, Spring 2017; William Voegeli, "The Democratic Party's Identity Crisis," *Claremont Review of Books*, Winter 2016/17. See also William McGurn, "Why Elites Hate," *Wall Street Journal*, June 5, 2017.

opposed "with manly firmness" George the Third's "invasions on the rights of the people."[43] And inspired by their example,

> the Representatives of the united States of America . . . appealing to the Supreme Judge of the world for the rectitude of our intentions, do, in the Name, and by Authority of the good People of these Colonies, solemnly publish and declare, That these united Colonies are, and of Right ought to be Free and Independent States.

Given human nature, Resistance partisans will be inclined to ascribe to their own attitude and activities vis-à-vis Trump the positive features of representative bodies (minus, no doubt, the ascription of manliness). However, that is not the issue at hand: it is Trump as representative. To maintain that he does not represent their views does not entail that his representation is *ipso facto* illegitimate. He may represent another group of Americans. What about their right to be represented? Is that contested too? The typical halfway answer—"n-es," "no-and-yes"—quite literally wants it both ways. Events on college campuses and elsewhere, typically occurring under the banner of "cancel culture," indicate what happens when the charade ends. We see the exclusionary binary—"legitimate/illegitimate"—that Manent observed in Europe, this time at work here.[44]

On the other hand, if members of the Resistance want to put themselves in the hero role, then consistency requires the application of the full set of criteria sketched by the Declaration in

---

43 Just before this passage, it referred to "the right of Representation in the Legislature, a right inestimable to them and formidable to tyrants only."

44 Not a year later, Andrew Sullivan famous wrote, "We all live on campus now." https://nymag.com/intelligencer/2018/02/we-all-live-on-campus-now.html.

connection with authentic "Representatives." Do they see themselves as under God? As bound to observe His laws and moral norms? From what "good People" do they draw their authorization? Or is it rather self-authorization? Manent's observation suggests that this worldview tends to circumscribe the notion of democracy in a way that is both exclusionary and self-validating. If true, that would be very troubling, indicating a house dividing. Or more precisely: a house already divided in principle by the Resistance.[45]

As for the illegitimate exercise of legitimate authority, the Declaration brings to the world's attention the "abuses and usurpations" of executive power which, taken together, indicate a "Design" leading to "Absolute Despotism." But in so doing, it provides an extensive template for detecting and measuring such possible tyrannical designs. To make good its *claims*, the Resistance would have to make an actual *case* and *make good its case* in the court of public opinion. Mere charges, mere denunciations, mere epithets, are not the Declaration's way; indeed, they are the antithesis of the Declaration's way.

This brings us to the existential threat that purportedly justifies not mere opposition, but Resistance. The Declaration makes clear that a threat of this kind justifies *revolution*. Is that where the Resistance wishes to go—or, better put, where its principles and worldview lead? I am reminded of Edmund Burke's observation that the first revolution occurs in the minds of men. What indeed is the Resistance thinking?

---

45 Subsequent actions by the Democratic Party and its allies in federal agencies made this possibility a chilling reality. This included the weaponization of the FBI and DOJ against political opponents (as well as obstructing justice for political patrons and their sons). See Chapter Eighteen.

Chapter Nine

Habent sua fata libelli—books have their fate—goes a classical adage. Website essays do as well. At the time the previous essay was published (July 4, 2017), *Law and Liberty* maintained a "Comments" option. The essay, including its enigmatic ending, struck a nerve—indeed several—with its readers. After trying to respond to them in the combox, I decided that I needed to explain at greater length my thinking about Resistance thinking, which often went under the banner of "identity politics" and contemporary "Progressivism." Thanks to the indulgence of the editors at *Law and Liberty*, in the span of one month (August 1–30) I published six essays, the first entitled "What Are They Thinking?" and the second "Progressivism in the Resistance." With them, I began a long exposition of the thinking that so immediately resisted President Trump, seeing in him an existential threat.

WHAT ARE THEY THINKING? (2017)

Recently, I raised the issue of the worldview of the Resistance to President Trump. I would like to delve further into the matter. It will take several installments. Basically, what I hope to do is to put in order some readings, observations, impressions, and overhearings. (As for the latter category, I live in a university neighborhood in Baltimore and one establishment I frequent is the aptly named "One World Café," where I am regularly regaled by unvarnished progressive opining.) This effort is neither scientific nor exhaustive. Call it "political" in the sense Pierre Manent employs when he says *les choses politiques arrivent en gros* ("political things first come to sight in rough outline").

I take as my starting point a widely shared observation: that the Democratic Party, a chief organ of Resistance, is wedded to identity politics, especially a secular trinity of race, sex, and gender. William Voegeli, for example, says that the party is in the "grip" of "identity liberalism,"[46] and he locates that trinity at the core of a moral-political vision of "diversity, multiculturalism, and inclusivity" that constitutes *its* identity.

Racial Identity

Race is a good starting point. Ferguson, Missouri, the subsequent campus protests, and the emergence of Black Lives Matter as a powerful force, bring us into a third phase of modern liberalism's dealing with the shameful history and legacy of slavery and segregation. First there was LBJ's landmark Civil Rights legislation and Hubert Humphrey's well-intentioned version of affirmative action (outreach seeking to widen the pool of qualified candidates, together with a promise "to eat [his] hat" if it became racial quotas). Affirmative action, however, did become quotas, set-asides, and demands for proportional representation, in part (but only in part) because of the slow pace of improvement yielded under the original policy. Liberalism thus entered a decidedly different phase, where formal equality and equality of opportunity were to be replaced by "real equality" and measurable results. "Diversity" became a mantra, a required goal, and, in many instances, a cudgel. Many grifters such as Al Sharpton learned the art of the racial shake-down.

Even that, however, has proven unsatisfactory to many, and we now have a yet more encompassing view of race in America

---

46 https://claremontreviewofbooks.com/the-democratic-partys-identity-crisis/.

encapsulated in phrases such as "white privilege," expressed by writers such as Ta-Nehisi Coates and Robin DiAngelo, and found in the Black Lives Matter "Guiding Principles." The words "systematic" and "racism" are joined and America, past and present, is condemned as a whole (with precious few exceptions): entire segments of the non-black population and many institutions are indicted for their current racist *being*, not just their (purported or real) retrograde views. Connected as these charges are with ideas of *structural* injustice, passionate demands for sweeping changes naturally flow from them.

The Resistance uneasily combines the second and third positions, with the latest version providing new energy and arrogating to itself the radical moral high ground. Partisans and beneficiaries of the earlier revised version may see them as useful shock troops, while casting themselves as soberer heads more in tune with the ways of the world. But at the very least they are tactical allies. As for what will eventuate between the two, no one knows, but revolutions devouring their own is not out of the question. Possible too is "mainstreaming" the radical view; indeed, there is considerable evidence that this is already occurring.

Be that as it may, for the foreseeable future both cohorts will turn demanding racialized gazes upon their country and their fellow citizens and predictably, necessarily, will see what they are predetermined to see: systematic racial inequalities due (they say) to racist ideas, ill-begotten institutions, and invidious legacies.

Sexual Identity

After race, sex and gender are central to this worldview, perhaps more fundamental than race, at least in some ways. The list of recent telling phenomena is well-known: Arizona and Indiana, with then-Governors Brewer and Pence subject to intense pressure to scuttle modest religious protections modeled after federal law;

Obergefell mandating same-sex marriage; and North Carolina regulating public bathrooms in a traditional way and the NCAA threatening to take its tournaments and dollars away from it and all states embodying such "bigotry." As I said, here we are onto something that is at the vital core of the Resistance mentality, even sacred to it. In the Supreme Court *Ur*-decision in this area, *Griswold v. Connecticut*, William O. Douglas intimated a (D. H.) Lawrencian religion of the sanctity of sex,[47] one that subsequent court decisions have ratified and expanded, with Justice Kennedy become the poet-jurist of the unquestionable dignity of expressive intimacy in *Lawrence v. Texas* and *Obergefell.*

Sexuality and gender are generally viewed through bifocals combining the categories of "nature" and "social convention," but always showing up as matter for the individual self, not to be subject to any public criterion of judgment, save that of consent. Correlated to this positive view of human sexuality and gender as strictly matters of equality and freedom understood in their most egalitarian and emancipatory senses is antipathy toward anyone who explicitly *or even inferentially* does not share these individualistic and morally homogenizing views. So-called "traditional views" of sexuality, marriage, and family, and their typical supports, traditional religions, are *l'infâme* to be, if not crushed, legally brought to heel and socially shamed. On this score, one can read Justice Alito's dissent in *Obergefell*,

---

47 Douglas employed the term "sacred" twice in the decision: first, in the famous phrase "sacred precincts of the marital bedroom," then later: "intimate to the degree of being sacred." The first alluded to the traditional understanding of human sexuality, the monogamous marital union and its "noble purpose," the second (please note) *derived sacredness from sexual intimacy.* The latter, however, was not circumscribed by object, purpose, circumstance, or duration. Douglas exploited the prestige of the former to bring in and justify the latter. Subsequent decisions (*Eisenstadt; Roe; Lawrence*) jettisoned the marital fig-leaf.

or ask progressive legal scholar Chai Feldblum and LGBTQ financial backer and strategist Tim Gill their views.[48] The former has "a hard time coming up with any case in which religious liberty should win," while the latter declares, "We're going to punish the wicked."[49] More positively, sexual and gender minorities that historically were subject to legal sanction and moral disapprobrium are not only to be legally protected (a welcome development), but also publicly celebrated and incorporated as estimable models in educational curricula and the workplace. The Starbucks I go to is a good example of welcomed and patronized sexual diversity. Pride flags and rainbows plastered on the walls of elementary school classrooms, a much more worrisome one.[50]

Tocqueville and Durkheim

This progressive attitude towards sex and gender can be understood in Tocquevillian and Durkheimian terms. The French political thinker presciently noted that the democratic principles of equality, freedom, and consent would tend to radicalize themselves over the course of democracy's history, both in intension and extension. Equality and freedom would become detached from substantive content and traditional norms and egalitarian consent would gain the whip-hand

48 https://www.law.cornell.edu/supct/pdf/14-556.pdf.
49 Feldblum: "I'm having a hard time coming up with any case in which religious liberty should win." Quoted by Maggie Gallagher, "Banned in Boston," *The Weekly Standard*, May 15, 2006. Gill: "We're going to punish the wicked." Andy Kroll, "Meet the Megadonor Behind the LGBTQ Rights Movement," *Rolling Stone*, June 23, 2017.
50 One can go to the Libs of TikTok (https://twitter.com/libsoftiktok) to see constantly updated examples of the sexual confusion, perversion, duplicity, and machinations of promoters of minority "Pride," "gender fluidity," and "gender affirmation" in the classroom.

in private and social matters, once they were enthroned in the authoritative political realm. In today's public discourse about human sexuality, it is striking how often obvious biological and moral distinctions are denied or obscured, treated as *personae non gratae*, and those who attempt to bring them into the conversation are accused of "bigotry" and other anti-egalitarian sins. This obtuseness starts with the most obvious facts of heterosexual intercourse's potential procreativity and homosexual sex's intrinsic sterility, and go to social science's clear findings about what sexual arrangement—what social institution—is best for children: a low degree of conflict heterosexual marriage. There is a(n a)moral dogmatism at work here, a prevenient vision of right and fact that is deeply resistant to relevant evidence and counter argument. Tocquevillian categories can help explain this resistance.

As for the sociologist Durkheim, he pointed out that even modern society would have its "sacred." In Christopher Smith's formulation,

> [b]y "sacred," I mean things set apart from the profane and forbidden to be violated, exactly what the sociologist Emile Durkheim meant by the term. Sacred matters are never ordinary, mundane, or instrumental. They are reverenced, venerated, and defended as sacrosanct by the social groups that hold them as sacred…. Sacred objects are hallowed, revered, and honored as beyond questioning or disrespect.[51]

Banishing Socrates

The foregoing phrase ("beyond questioning") indicates why Socrates is not welcome when it comes to modern *eros*. In the

51 Christopher Smith, *The Sacred Project of American Sociology* (Oxford University Press, 2014), p. 1.

domain of sexuality and gender, all too often magic words such as "love," "equality," "choice," and "fluidity" substitute for substantive argument or even thought. And the fundamental act of reasoning, making distinctions, is *a priori* suspected of being "invidious" and "judgmental"—and, as evidenced by vehement reactions, profaning something *sacred*.

The ban placed on rational inquiry and candid discussion in this area of human life, with its tremendous importance for personal happiness and social stability and continuity, is a cause for very grave concern, both because of the strictures it places on reason itself and because of the obfuscation of human sexuality involved, which is particularly disorienting to young people. Indeed, there is reason to believe this is intentional. Insofar as it is wedded to this view, therefore, the Resistance is an enemy of the precious human faculty, reason, and disserves what it claims to champion, human sexuality in its complexity. Dogmatism always does that, even—or perhaps especially—when done in the name of democracy's core values.

Chapter Ten

Having begun with the Democratic Party's commitment to its sacred trinity of "race, sex, and gender," the circle needed to be expanded to Progressivism and its characteristic attitude toward two great instances, the Constitution and religion.

PROGRESSIVISM IN THE RESISTANCE (2017)

In a first installment ("Resistance in the Light of 1776"), following the lead of Pierre Manent, the Resistance came into sight as a way of looking at things characterized by 1) a binary view of legitimate and illegitimate views (in keeping with Hillary Clinton's "racist, sexist, homophobic, xenophobic, Islamophobic—you name it" litany); 2) a quasi-religious cast ("political orthodoxy and heresy"); and 3) a novel form of democracy characterized by terms such as "diversity," "multiculturalism," and "inclusion," but with its own blind spots and exclusions. As I put it: it is "rather exclusive in its inclusivity and monolithic in its view of diversity."

A second installment ("What Are They Thinking?") focused on the moral core of the worldview, the secular trinity of race, sex, and gender. The Resistance view of black and white America casts a harsh, demanding Manichean gaze on the country and its white citizens, while its latitudinarian view of human sexuality and gender can be understood in Tocquevillian and Durkheimian terms. Over time, as Tocqueville foresaw, democracy's principles of equality and freedom have been radicalized, that is, emptied of substantive content and extended to more and more of reality (in this case, human sexuality); given that this extension is conducted in the name of democracy's sacred values of equality and freedom, to question an extension and its legitimacy is tantamount to profanation (hence Durkheim). In the first case, the older liberal view of equality under law is seen as a pretext for malign neglect (think "Critical Race Theory"), while in the latter area, Socrates and his probing question are banished from the public discussion of *eros*. Sturdy modernity and classical thought share a common fate.

Religion and the Constitution

During the course of the second reflection, religion (especially in its traditional forms) and the Constitution came up; traditional religion as an object of deep antipathy to the Resistance because of its benighted and "bigoted" view of human sexuality, the Constitution as invoked by the Supreme Court in its privacy and dignity jurisprudence, which has done so much to further the sexual revolution. As the Resistance views them, these two subjects merit further consideration.

Higher Guidance, or Malleable Instruments?

The Constitution, of course, is the American framing document, while religion is a significant part of the lives of many Americans, an important social presence. While different, the two are not simply separate phenomena, witness the First Amendment and recent Supreme Court decisions (*Hosanna-Tabor, Burwell v. Hobby Lobby, Trinity Lutheran*). More importantly, both present themselves as existing above ordinary democratic will, as providing settled norms and forms that allow for communal progress and human flourishing. They are part of the "what we look up to" of our democracy.

The Resistance has a particular take on both, dictated by its moral commitments and its core progressivism. It tends to instrumentalize the two instances and to judge them by external criteria, thus depriving them of their distinct contributions to our democracy. Both instances indeed elevate free and democratic selves, but they also indicate salutary limits to freedom, but only if viewed in their proper natures. The sociologist James Davison Hunter captured important aspects of this instrumentalizing worldview in his 1991 study, *Culture Wars: The Struggle to Define America*, under the rubric of the "Progressive" impulse (which pits itself against the "Orthodox").[52]

While Hunter does not say so, the Progressive attitude exemplifies Tocqueville's earlier twin fears of democratic "pantheism" (or immanentism) and historicism. According to Hunter, the Progressive worldview locates ultimate "moral authority," not in a transcendent instance (the Biblical God or a normative Nature), but in humanity itself. Moreover, humankind is situated in a progressive view of History: the democratic age succeeded the aristocratic and the democratic age will become progressively more so. Finally, in the Progressive worldview humanity and History join in "the spirit of the times." The modern *Zeitgeist*, it is said, is committed to the twin lodestars of "scientific rationality" and individual "autonomy." Science debunks myths and prejudices, as well as empowers human will, while autonomy is the effectual truth of human dignity and the main criterion of social progress. All this enters into the Resistance view of things. For example, the monkey wrench which was the election of Donald Trump and the seismic shock it caused in the Resistance psyche indicate how ingrained the progressive view of history was, especially after eight years of President Obama.

52 *Culture Wars: The Struggle to Define America* (Basic Books, 1991).

When it comes to religion, the Resistance necessarily harbors hostility toward traditional religion, because of the latter's refusal to go along with its sexual and gender views, but also because of its purported variance from ScienceTM.[53] More ominously, orthodox religion is seen as a threat to democracy itself, to be kept at bay, if not disqualified from public life. Bernie Sanders and Chris Van Hollen recently displayed this hard-edged prejudice against religious beliefs that do not comport with progressive views of human equality and democracy.[54] Before them, we heard the blunt declaration of Julian Castro, the Chairman of the U. S. Commission on Civil Rights in the Obama administration: "The phrases 'religious liberty' and 'religious freedom' will stand for nothing except hypocrisy so long as they as they remain code words for discrimination, intolerance, racism, sexism, homophobia, Islamophobia or any form of intolerance."[55]

53 Admittedly, there is low-hanging fruit to be plucked in this area (e.g., Ken Ham and his Creation Museum), but generally speaking the progressive Resistance is woefully ignorant of the faiths they critique and the relevant work on faith and science (and philosophy and theology) of thinkers such as Joseph Ratzinger, Alvin Plantinga, Robert Spitzer, Stephen Barr, Michael Hanby, and many others. From time to time, I talk with Ph.D. candidates at Johns Hopkins University in both the sciences and the humanities and am astounded at their ignorance, errors, and arrogance in these areas. However, I am also inclined to think to myself when I do, "Father, forgive them, for they know not what they are talking about. They've never encountered genuinely learned faith in their milieux." This is yet another scandal attached to contemporary higher education.
54 https://www.nationalreview.com/corner/watch-bernie-sanders-unconstitutionally-impose-religious-test-public-office/. Later, in 2020, Democratic Senator Diane Feinstein expressed concern that "the dogma lives loudly" in then-nominee Amy Comey Barrett.
55 https://religionnews.com/2016/09/08/chairman-of-u-s-commission-on-civil-rights-calls-the-phrases-religious-liberty-and-religious-freedom-code-words-for-discrimination-intolerance-racism-s/.

"Nothing"? The secular litany of taboos is now to be the criterion for judging religious claims and exercise.

To be sure, *progressive* believers and denominations are welcome and many of them are part of the Resistance.

The Living Constitution

Given its progressive view of History, it almost goes without saying that the Resistance views the Constitution as "a living document." Another way of putting the point was voiced by the medieval dictum that "Authority has a nose of wax [i.e., is easy to twist to one's desire]." Judicial decisions are commended or not according to their consonance with progressive moral and political desiderata. Thus, the privacy and dignity jurisprudence of the past fifty years is hailed and the Supreme Court lionized as a bastion of individual liberty. On the other hand, President Obama's critiquing the *Citizens United* decision during a State of the Union address indicates that the Court can err in its historical mission. Then it needs to be lectured from the bully pulpit by one who knows the arc of History.

Indeed, ambivalence runs throughout this mentality when it comes to constitutional matters and forms. In his book *Rush to Judgment*, presidential scholar Steve Knott has shown how the phrase "the imperial presidency" was coined to indict Richard Nixon's presidency, but is held in abeyance when progressive chief executives hold office.[56] In general, since the clear and present danger to the Republic today is located in the executive office, the Resistance looks to members of the other two branches to resist. Early

---

56 *Rush to Judgment: George W. Bush, the War on Terror, and His Critics* (The University Press of Kansas, 2012). One can consult my review: https://www.tandfonline.com/doi/full/10.1080/10457097.2014.90 0327.

federal court decisions staying the Trump administration's travel ban, despite departing egregiously from settled rules of construction and previous rulings, were hailed as victories for "the Constitution" and "democracy." Likewise, while progressives once were deeply suspicious of "the deep state," the Resistance has discovered unsuspected virtues and work for it in these harrowing circumstances. Subsequent revelations of egregious misconduct by Peter Strzok, Lisa Page, Kevin Clinesmith, James Comey, John Brennan, and innumerable others in our alphabet intelligence and security agencies demonstrated just how much that newly placed trust was well-founded.[57]

---

57   See note 45 above and note 70 below.

Chapter Eleven

While I covered significant ground in the previous reflections, other topics relevant to understanding the Resistance had not been discussed. For example, Muslims entered into the Resistance view of religion, as well as of immigration and citizenship. Why was "xenophobia" so readily attached to restrictionist policies by the Trump administration when they basically followed a list created by the Obama administration? Why was the Resistance so sensitive to Islamophobia at home when, in important respects, any number of Islam's traditions and customs were antithetical to it? I therefore needed to broaden the horizon of our study. In the final analysis, Resistance draws its moral authority from its view of Humanity (with a capital "H"). It is Humanity's defender against its divisive enemies, not just Donald Trump, but those who put country or particular people above Humanity.

THE RELIGION OF HUMANITY (2017)

We can't help it, we're human, we necessarily have worldviews. Everybody does. The Resistance does too, rough-hewn, in the aggregate, and tacit as it may be. Now it is time to take a look squarely at the Resistance's main object of concern: humanity itself. The Resistance declares itself "inclusive" and it hates "exclusion." Its vision and concern encompass all of humankind. But not all humanisms are created equal. Who is to say that Resistance humanitarianism is unquestionable? Not me. Not Pierre Manent.

Revealing Phenomena

Following my usual procedure, I begin with telling phenomena, revealing signs of the underlying humanitarian vision of the Resistance. Any talk of immigration restriction is declared (or suspected of being) "racist" and "xenophobic" and temporary bans on immigration from predominantly Muslim countries with known inabilities to vet Islamist terrorists are automatically judged "Islamophobic." As a rule, greater public concern is shown for possible "backlash" against Muslims here than for the victims of terrorist murder. Typically, the condemnation of such murder is ritualistic, conveyed in flat tones, and then dropped so as not to give aid and comfort to the real enemy, domestic political opponents who are "Islamophobic" and "anti-immigrant." The binary character of Resistance thinking thus shows itself again, precisely in the assertion and defense of its inclusive view of humanity.

Islam and Muslims are a striking exception to Progressive-Resistance general antipathy toward sexually stringent traditional religions, so they are a particularly revealing case of its expansive "openness" and aversion to "exclusion." To be sure, Muslims are often defended on the tactical principle of "the enemy of my enemy is my ally." But there is something deeper here at work, and, once again, Pierre Manent can help bring it to light. It is precisely a certain sort of humanitarianism, one with a capital H.[58]

58 Manent distinguishes the type of humanitarianism he has in mind, what he calls "the religion of Humanity," from that practiced, for example, by *Doctors without Borders.* "Humanitarian action, properly speaking, for example, medical assistance, is perfectly praiseworthy and I only have admiration for the French doctors of *Doctors without Borders* who practice it." "The Humanitarian Temptation," in *The Religion of Humanity* (St. Augustine Press, 2022), p. 35.

The Religion of Humanity

Here too (as he had with the new understanding of democracy), Manent had the dubious privilege of observing its European version long before the Resistance declared against Trump. In a shorthand formulation, it is a view—an image, an idea— of humanity as already, or virtually, unified, with no significant differences to scuttle human unity.[59] Anyone who merely points out obvious differences and divisions that exist among human beings is taken to *endorse* them, to delight in human division, and to be in the grips of *odium unitatis generis humani*. Anyone who says that these differences in beliefs and morals and collective organization and patterns of behavior are humanly significant and merit discussion, both civic and philosophic, has deliberately, with ill intent, opened a can of worms and troubled the desirable unity of humanity.

59 "[T]he image of a virtually unified humanity," *A World beyond Politics? A Defense of the Nation-State* (Princeton University Press, 2006), p. 178. "[A] vague idea of human unity, an imminent unity that would resolve by a kind of internal necessity that problem of human order." *Democracy Without Nations?* (ISI Books, 2007), p. 6. An idea, an image, it is also a mandated belief, as the text above reports. Finally, it is an actively pursued suppression or denial: "Since every *significant* collective difference puts human unity in danger, one must render every difference *insignificant*." *Democracy without Nations?*, p. 8 (italics in the original). Cf. "the religion of Humanity, which is the contemporary religion of Europe and of the West, forbids us from distinguishing seriously among groups of human beings. The 'right to be different' means only the prohibition from *seeing* differences." *Seeing Things Politically* (St. Augustine Press, 2015), trans. by Ralph C. Hancock, Introduction by Daniel J. Mahoney, p. 172 (italics original)). For a fuller treatment of Manent's view of this ersatz humanitarian religion, see the anthology *The Religion of Humanity* cited in the previous note. One could also consult my "What is the Religion of Humanity?" (https://lawliberty.org/what-is-the-religion-of-humanity/).

On the European continent, this view had taken on the form of a secular religion, "a religion of Humanity," one that was strictly enforced in their version of political correctness. In 2010, Manent wrote:

> According to this public philosophy, we see, we *must* see, we *can only* see, human unity, or at least humanity in the process of unification. But if we claim to see what we do not see, if what is visible, and what is visibly fragmented, do not arrest our gaze, and if, on the contrary, we *believe* we are seeing *the invisible unity of humanity*, then we are indeed part of what we can only call a religion, part of what I am happy to call, following others, "the religion of Humanity." We are not only under the power of an idea; rather, the philosophical idea of humanity comes along with a religious enthusiasm (italics added).[60]

As a political philosopher, Manent analyzed this ersatz religion's characteristics and sources, as well as various domains in which it displayed itself (international law, identity politics, moral relativism), subjecting it to philosophical and political critique. Some of these analyses possessed the guilty pleasure of exhibiting his capacity for sarcasm. One piquant example:

> Under a flashing neon sign proclaiming "human unity," contemporary Europeans would have humanity arrest all intellectual or spiritual movement in order to conduct a continual, interminable liturgy of self-adoration.[61]

60 *Seeing Things Politically*, pp. 151–52.
61 *Democracy without Nations?*, pp. 8–9.

The point was serious though, as it indicated the "atheistic humanism" involved, as well as its stifling self-satisfaction. Whereas premodern Europeans were often involved in the great adventures of *searching for* philosophical and religious *truth* and were alive to the human possibility of "conversion," of aligning one's soul with the truth found or accepted, contemporary European democrats deemed themselves safely beyond those adventures and challenges. A certain "democratic complacency" was publicly enshrined on the continent, one born of dogmatic skepticism compounded by easygoing self-affirmation.

Relativistic Dignity

Its centerpiece, according to Manent, was a distinctive view of human *dignity*, the central category of "contemporary moral consciousness." It was Kant who most powerfully put human dignity on the modern philosophical map. Manent's main points about today's understanding bore upon the "democratization" of Kant's sterner understanding and the new version's affront to the natural movements of the human spirit—and hence to Socrates. Today,

> to respect the dignity of other human beings is no
> longer to respect the respect they hold within themselves for the moral law [that was Kant's view]. Today it
> is more to respect the choice they have made, whatever
> that choice may be, in asserting their rights. For Kant,
> respect for human dignity is respect for humanity itself;
> for contemporary moralism, respect for human dignity
> is respect for the "contents of life," whatever it may be,
> of other human beings. The same words are used, but
> with an altogether different moral perspective.[62]

62 *A World beyond Politics?*, p. 193.

According to the Kantian perspective,

> My respect is addressed to the humanity of the other human beings; as human beings they are essentially respectable. Now, what they do with their life, the "contents of their life," is another thing; I can approve, disapprove, be indifferent, or be perplexed, in short, here the full scale of feelings and judgments that life arouses in us is naturally deployed.[63]

In the Kantian dispensation, the human mind is still given free rein to follow its natural movements. And Socrates can ask his probing questions, even in the public square.

The contemporary public square is quite different, however. There, "[r]espect is demanded for all life contents, all life choices, or all lifestyles."[64]

But, observed Manent,

> [t]his formulation really has no meaning. Or its only meaning is that all life contents, all life choices, all lifestyles must be approved, appreciated, valued, applauded. But that is simply impossible.[65]

With the magic wand of this indiscriminate notion of dignity, everything is dignified. But most human beings know that everything is not dignified, that ideas and choices and beliefs and sexual practices and orientations and notions of justice and nobility are not self-justifying or even self-explanatory. The Socratic imperative of "giving an account" (*logon didonai*) still continues (if weakly)

63 *Ibid.*
64 *Ibid.*, p. 194.
65 *Ibid.*

for human beings in advanced democratic times. In denying this, contemporary moralism is deeply anti-philosophic, at war with the reality of human beings and the human mind.

Nor will it do to say that public law can be a blanket licensing of lifestyles, while civil society and private life can continue their judging ways. The classics and Tocqueville taught that what is authoritative in the political realm becomes authoritative *tout court*. This is often on display here in America. Take the Supreme Court and Justice Kennedy.

Justice Kennedy

After Justice William Brennan (1906–1997), Kennedy is the one who has most promoted this catch-all view of human dignity in our jurisprudence.[66] From the "sweet mystery of life" in *Planned Parenthood v. Casey* (1992) to his setting up of two opposed "legislative bodies" in *Lawrence v. Texas* (2003)—the autonomous individual and state legislatures—and declaring that the dignified autonomous self cannot be judged or limited by morals legislation, we in America know this heavy-handed application of relativistic dignity. Its extension to same-sex marriage in *Obergefell v. Hodges* (2015) was a foregone conclusion, but not *the* conclusion, of the position's logic. Contemplating these latter prospects, reason and moral sense shudder.

What about US?

The example of Justice Kennedy reminds us that the inclusive humanitarianism of American progressivism, while sharing many

66 For a magisterial dissection of Brennan's jurisprudence, see Robert K. Faulkner, "Difficulties of Equal Dignity: The Court and the Family," in *The Constitution, the Courts, and the Quest for Justice* (AEI Press, 1988).

features with its European cousin, is also different because of unique features of the American scene. For example, we have already spoken about the central place and role that African Americans occupy in its views of race and country. In the face of Manent's insistence that the normative unity of Humanity is the core of this worldview (at the price of failing to take seriously serious human differences), some readers will have wondered where the Resistance's normative insistence on "diversity" and (select) "minorities" fits in?   In the face of questions like these, there is a need to turn to more America-focused analyses of this sort of cosmopolitan humanitarianism. Happily, one is available.

Chapter Twelve

While Manent is an incisive European political philosopher, we Americans need American help in understanding our progressives' version of Humanity and History. Fortunately, there was someone who had recognized the American phenomenon early on, John Fonte of the Hudson Institute. He published his analysis in a famous 2002 article.

TRANSNATIONAL PROGRESSIVISM AND THE US (2017)

John Fonte's groundbreaking analysis of a new version of humanitarianism details its privileging of racial, ethnic, and gender categories and divisions in its vision of humanity. He refers to it as "Transnational Progressivism." It is very much an American phenomenon (although with European collaborators, as we might suspect).

Fonte's 2002 article, "Liberal Democracy versus Transnational Progressivism: The Future of the Ideological Civil War Within the West,"[67] begins with his own eye-opening phenomenon: the 2001 "United Nations World Conference against Racism, Racial Discrimination, Xenophobia, and Related Intolerance" held in Durban, South Africa, shortly before 9/11. Fonte was struck by the following: In the run-up to the conference, about 50 (!) American

---

67   John Fonte, "Liberal Democracy vs. Transnational Progressivism: The Future of Ideological Civil War within the West," *Orbis*, Summer 2002.

NGOs, including some of the most prominent and well-funded, petitioned Mary Robinson, then UN Human Rights Commissioner, to have the United Nations compel the United States to address "the intractable and persistent problem of racism" that "men and women of color face at the hands of the U.S. criminal justice system." They thereby sought to subordinate the institutions, processes, and results of American self-government to a higher instance. This was quite arresting and intriguing.

Then during the conference itself, the same NGOs produced a series of "demands" on the United States that, collectively, would entail that the country "would have to turn its political and economic system, together with their underlying principles, upside-down—abandoning the free speech guarantees of the Constitution, bypassing federalism, and ignoring the very concept of majority rule—because practically nothing in the NGO agenda is supported by the American electorate."

All in all, he had discovered something new, coordinated, and potentially revolutionary: a new political vision and agenda for America and the world. It was, to say the least, worth further study. In time, he gave it a name, "transnational progressivism," and penned the eponymous article, "Liberal Democracy versus Transnational Progressivism," foreseeing a coming "civil war" at home and abroad. It is not implausible to see the Resistance, as a noun, as combatants in that war, and as a verbal noun, a battle in it. Let's head down that road.

Transnational Progressivism's Worldview

Fonte sums up this worldview or "ideology" in nine traits. His discussion of each is prefaced by an italicized thesis-phrase or statement. Here is that list: 1) *The ascribed group over the individual.* 2) *A dichotomy of groups: Oppressor versus victim groups, with immigrant groups designated as victims.* 3) *Group proportionalism as the goal of "fairness." 4) The values of all dominant institutions to be changed to reflect the perspective of the victim groups. 5) The Demographic Imperative.* (By this he means the view that, because of domestic demographic changes and global population flows, "the traditional paradigm of American nationhood [is] obsolete" and "must be changed into a system that promotes 'diversity,' defined, in the end, as group proportionalism"). *6) The redefinition of democracy and "democratic ideals." 7) Deconstruction of national narratives and national symbols. 8) Promotion of the concept of postnational citizenship. 9) The idea of transnationalism as a major conceptual tool.*

There is a great deal in this sketch of the transnational progressive ideology (TPI), including elements we have seen in previous chapters. It will take a couple of chapters to unpack them. The major new element is "groups," which figure in various ways as the prime unit of analysis. The novelty of the configuration they will form is indicated by the telling prefixes "trans-" and "post-." This is progressivism marching forward to a new world order. The loaded terms "oppressor and oppressed," not to mention "fairness," indicate that the vision is far from realized, that it is fueled by indignation at current and past injustice, and that it claims justice as its justification. In all these ways, it is a prime candidate for political philosophical analysis and critique. I will begin with three elements we have seen in previous installments: "preferences"; the trinity of "race, ethnicity, and gender"; and binary thinking, now become a "dichotomy of groups."

Group Preferences

In the TPI optic, "equality under the law is replaced by legal preferences for traditionally victimized groups." We saw this earlier with the betrayal of Hubert Humphrey's promise "to eat [his] hat" if affirmative action became "quotas." Now, however, the "victimized" groups have multiplied; they no longer are only African

Americans, or even only racially defined, and the head-counting demanded by "proportional representation" requires the "materialization" of the various qualities (racial, ethnic, sexual, cultural) making for a distinctive group. Qualia have to be cast as quanta for the scheme to be operational.

Manent has pointed out that this quantification requires and produces a stable and static object, while Fonte adds that the individual is deemed to be ensconced in that group-set of characteristics and these characteristics are deemed the most important, the defining ones, for public purposes. True individuality, real individuals, thus suffer, as does—to return to Manent—the possibility of conversion, or of self-transcendence by participation in a higher common good. Racially mixed sports teams—to take a quintessential American example—belie this impossibility, of course. Indeed, all but ideologues (and cynical powerbrokers) know that the above claims are false to the reality of being human. We're not just our (purported, often fictional) group characteristics, we're not just our external markers. The TPI lens terribly reduces and skews human reality and hence undermines human flourishing and community.

This last point raises the issue of what can be "common" in this groups-focused mode of analysis? What form, or forms, of community can such groups pursue, achieve, and share? One form of community, admittedly rather external, is having a common enemy. The language of "oppressor" and "oppressed," of "victim" (and thus "victimizers"), makes that possibility quite actual.

The Great Binary

Earlier, William Voegeli introduced us to the trinity of "race, sex, and gender" informing the Democratic Party's identity. Fonte also recognizes their centrality for this broader transnational ideology. He writes of individuals being assigned to an "ascriptive group (racial, ethnic, and gender)" in the ideology's optic, of its overriding "emphasis on race, ethnicity, and gender."

However, despite the necessary multiplicity (and ongoing multiplication) involved in considering humankind in terms of racial, ethnic, sexual, and gender groupings, another number—two—tends to trump, or finally define, them. Once again we encounter the binary thinking characteristic of Resistance thinking, now cast in terms of a "dichotomy of groups." At this important juncture of his argument, Fonte invokes what Aristotle called "the architectonic discipline," political philosophy, and one of its most expert contemporary practitioners, James Ceaser. "As the political philosopher James Ceaser puts it, multiculturalism is not 'multi,' concerned with many groups, but 'binary,' concerned with two groups, the hegemon (bad) and 'the Other' (good) or the oppressor and the oppressed." To Ceaser's decisive observation, Fonte adds a bit of intellectual genealogy. TPI did not appear *ex nihilo*.

To begin with, "in a certain sense, transnationalism is the next phase of multicultural ideology—it is multiculturalism with a global face." But merely recognizing a global context and its impact on the many cultural groups of humankind does not generate the full ideology. "Binary" must be added, indeed a binary of a certain sort, involving oppressors and oppressed. Fonte traces this key element and thought to "Hegelian Marxism," with its antecedents in the Master-slave dialectic of Hegel and embodiment in Marxist class analysis. "Cultural Marxism" picks up this form of thinking and substitutes "culture" for class. In connection with the latter, he provides the name of the Italian Marxist Antonio Gramsci *honoris causa* (although he cites other thinkers as well). His colleague at the Hudson Institute, Michael Gonzales, has further developed these leads in *The Plot to Change America: How Identity Politics Is Dividing the Land of the Free* (Encounter, 2020). Yasha Mounk more recently joined the lists of those exploring its genealogy with *The Identity Trap* (Penguin Press, 2023). Both are well worth reading.

A Brief Summary and Looking Forward

At this point, a broad sketch of TPI comes into view. In it, the past and the present are seen through 1) the frame of "culture" understood in racial, ethnic, sexual, and gender terms and categories, with 2) the overriding feature being their being assorted into two starkly opposed categories, those on top and those on the bottom (in Camus' classic phrase, "executioners and victims"). However, implicit in this dark Manichean view of History's dynamic structure is, *mirabile dictu*, a radiant Future that can be limned and pursued.[68]

However, this happy result will require present and ongoing warfare on multiple fronts. Between it and analyses of the past and the present, revolutionary strategies and tactics will have to be formulated and pursued.[69] Since it is warfare, a close analysis of the enemy is required. While "straight white males" are the demons (and previous drivers) of History, the institutional enemies are liberal democracy and the nation-state, especially their chief contemporary embodiment, America. In this revolutionary optic, resistance is *de rigueur* against anyone who claims to Make America Great

---

68   Fonte, however, does not take the time to sketch it. Among other things, one can anticipate that certain public musea and important portions of public education will be devoted to the shameful legacy of "dead white males" and of "white Christianity." A few statues of founding white males will be preserved from the foundry in order to be physical reminders of these infamous human beings for the generations to come. This will be all the more necessary as public schools will have removed their names.

69   The afore-mentioned Gramsci is an important figure in this regard, as was Herbert Marcuse in the American context. See the book by Gonzales mentioned above and the one by Rufo mentioned in the Introduction. A classic study of the subject is Roger Kimball, *Tenured Radicals* (Harpercollins, 1990).

Again, or who puts country and people above select racial or ethnic groups.

The battle against Trump goes far beyond his person, his program, and his followers, however. It wars against a set of ideas, a historical reality and project, and an intergenerational promise:

> We the People of the United States, in Order to form a more perfect Union, establish Justice, insure domestic Tranquility, provide for the common defence, promote the general Welfare, and secure the Blessings of Liberty to ourselves and our Posterity, do ordain and establish this Constitution for the United States of America.

It wars against America.

Chapter Thirteen

In modern ideology, the classical distinction between theory and practice undergoes radical transformation: it is cancelled and "sublimated." This recasting required a broader consideration of TPI. Put another way: revolutions need indoctrinating generals and indoctrinated troops.

THE BUSINESS END OF TRANSNATIONAL PROGRESSIVISM (2017)

According to John Fonte, "transnationalism is a concept that provides elites with both an empirical tool (a plausible analysis of what is) and an ideological framework (a vision of what should be)." What is, is humanity divided into groups along racial, ethnic, and gendered lines, with a fundamental line to be drawn between them, not in terms of spiritual or intellectual contributions to a common humanity, but rather between dominant and oppressed groups, victims and victimizers. Alas, not all groups or members of groups see themselves that way. Hence the reference to "elites" in the foregoing statement: they are the ones in possession of the requisite *gnosis*.

Fonte, accordingly, devotes a section to "Transnational Progressivism's Social Base: A Post-National Intelligentsia." While till now we have been more interested in its worldview than its institutional strongholds or individual proponents, a broader view necessarily includes all three.[70] His general statement reports that "the leaders … include many international law professors at prestigious Western universities, NGO activists, foundation officers, UN bureaucrats, EU administrators, corporate executives, and practicing politicians throughout the West."[71]

He also provides some particular names: sociologist Anthony Giddens, philosopher Martha Nussbaum, former diplomat Strobe Talbot, and the pair Toni Negri and Michael Hardt, Italian Marxist theorist and Duke University literature professor, respectively, who published the best-selling *Empire* in 2000. Each one can be taken, in Charles Péguy's apt phrase, as a *cas eminent*, an instance that illustrates a type, or a general attitude. The wholes thus exemplified can be a discipline in academe,[72] a type of diplomatic endeavor, innocuously entitled philanthropy and activism, and so on. They, however, should not be viewed in isolation. They form a more-or-less coherent "network."

Earlier, in connection with the Durban Conference, we saw how NGOs and major foundations collaborate. Thanks to Manent, we are not surprised to hear now that "EU administrators" are part of the network of collaborators, while Fonte adds "UN bureaucrats" to the list, again not a surprise. Fonte fills out his list with corporate captains and unnamed politicians, while Manent

70 See above, footnotes 57 & 70.

71 On the UN, two older books are still worth reading. Rosemary Righter, *Utopia Lost: The United Nations and World Order* (Brookings Institute Press, 1995) and on its specialized agency, the World Health Organization (WHO), see Richard E. Wagner & Robert D. Tollison, *Who Benefits from WHO?* (Social Affairs Unit, 1993). On WHO's compromised character and malfeasance in connection with the recent Covid response, see Kheriaty's *The New Abnormal.*

72 Fonte instances "the American Sociological Association." Christopher Smith would concur. See his *The Sacred Project of American Sociology* (Oxford University Press, 2014).

would add certain European jurists and courts.[73] Academe, business, politics, law, diplomacy, and activism—all have their transnational progressivists, all contribute to a network of "theory and practice." Well in place in America before the shock which was the electoral victory of Donald Trump, after that shock they are doing their best to make sure that no electoral defeat goes to waste. It is an opportunity for further recruitment and indoctrination of troops.

"Power-thought"

"Indoctrination" imposes itself as the term to use, but is perhaps too weak, because of the special character of the TPI worldview. It is theory *for the sake of practice*, it is intrinsically agenda-driven, starkly binary, and intentionally revolutionary. It aspires to be what Bertrand Russell called "power-thought."

As a result, designation on its part is *ipso facto* a call to indignation, resentment, and resistance on the part of some, or shame, repentance, and abnegation on the part of others. It is a constant *j'accuse*.[74] It has neither the character of Socratic *elenchus* (productive refutation), nor of Aristotle's equitable weaving together of the parts of the body politic by way of a consideration of various partial understandings of justice. Rather, it is presumptuous and contemptuous: presumptuous that it knows justice, contemptuous of those it identifies as privileged oppressors (or subjects of false consciousness). It is especially fueled by animus against enemies.

73 *A World beyond Politics?*, pp. 171–78; 186–87.
74 DEI sessions have rightly been likened to Maoist struggle sessions. For one recent account, see https://thefederalist.com/2023/12/28/bates-college-faculty-subjected-to-toxic-dei-struggle-sessions-by-administrators/.

Deconstructing the Enemy

The Enemy in America is tripartite, forming an unholy trinity: straight white Christian males; the fundamental institutions of America as a liberal democratic nation-state; and the national "symbols and narratives" that tacitly justify the rule of the white race and males, while explicitly appealing to some combination of Enlightenment thought (natural rights) and Protestant Christianity (the sanctity of individual conscience). Thought and culture are thus racialized and genderized, and human universalism is neither sought nor to be found. Rather, the national symbols and stories are to be "deconstructed" or "complicated," that is, unmasked and replaced.

Assimilation is therefore oppression, solely teaching English in public schools, a nefarious work of "erasure." Multilingualism must be the order of the day. Historical narratives must be broadened to include the contributions of all races, ethnicities, and genders to America. (Put that way, who could object?) But this must be done in the proper way: first, in the binary optic of oppression, and, second, with the aim of strictly equal billing, culturally speaking (at least for previous and current victim-groups). This sort of mandated equal status (in truth: egalitarian levelling) is, however, the antithesis of genuine culture and cultural development, as African American artists and critics—Ralph Ellison, Stanley Crouch—know perhaps better than most.[75] W. E. B. DuBois gave this truth a particularly beautiful expression.[76]

75   For Ellison, see *Going to the Territory*. For Crouch, see *The All-American Skin Game; or, The Decoy of Race: The Long and Short of It, 1990–1994*, as well as his obituary in the New York Times: https://www.nytimes.com/2020/09/16/obituaries/stanley-crouch-dead.html. Of his own intellectual development, he said: "I saw how important it is to free yourself from ideology. When you look at things solely in terms of race or class, you miss what is really going on."

76   "I sit with Shakespeare and he winces not. Across the color-line I

Something similar to what is demanded for "marginalized" cultures is called for at the political level. Proportional representation for the "disempowered" and "marginalized" must be guaranteed and groups as such must participate in new forms of "power sharing." Traditional practices of coalition-forming must be abandoned because based on the wrong sorts of identity or interests, and the character of democratic legitimacy and authority has to be recast. One must bid adieu to constitutionalism, majoritarianism, and national sovereignty.

National sovereignty must go because, with transnational progressivism, multiculturalism has gone global and humanitarianism is normative. Nations are to become open sites for migration and immigration, to be administrative units rather than self-determining political communities ("one node in a postnational network," said one proponent). From this vision arises a host of efforts to "reimagine" citizenship as "postnational," "transnational," and "global."

Topping things off would be some sort of "global governance" structure, involving or being served by "transnational organizations" and "transnational jurisprudence."[77] As Fonte indicated earlier, the EU and UN are anticipatory sketches, as well as suitable instruments, for the furthering of this goal.[78] Manent has pointed out that

move arm in arm with Balzac and Dumas, where smiling men and welcoming women glide in gilded halls. From out the caves of the evening that swing between the strong-limbed earth and the tracery of the stars, I summon Aristotle and Aurelius ... and they come all graciously with no scorn nor condescension. So, wed with Truth, I dwell above the Veil." *The Soul of Black Folks.*

77 Cf. Manent's treatment of "The Empire of Law" in *A World beyond Politics?*, pp. 178–87.

78 Since Covid, the important role of the World Health Organization in this effort has become clearer. So too has that of the World Economic Forum. For both of their globalist agendas, see Kheriaty's *The New Abnormal.*

"governance" is the preferred term of European elites, rather than "government" or "governing." The latter terms are still wedded to the archaic forms of national sovereignty and democratic self-rule, and they smack too much of authority, which means authoritarianism. The new humanitarian order requires a kinder, gentler term. Sometimes, though, it displays a steel hand within its velvet glove.

Summing Up

With Manent and Fonte, we have incisive critics of two versions of post-liberal democratic humanitarianism. The one analyzed by Manent is, in principle, rather soft, complacent, and welcoming, the one considered by Fonte, hard-edged and hard-driving. The former focuses much more on the individual,[79] while the latter is emphatically group-focused. The first believes humanity is in principle unified, with no significant differences to trouble us, the second maintains fundamental oppositions between groups and its theory is designed to expose and upend them. Reconciliation of the two would seem to be impossible.

Still, they have common enemies—the nation as a sovereign community, liberal democracy in its constitutional version—so they can, as often happens in war, make common cause while their enemy is still in the field. For example, soft humanitarianism informs a good deal of immigration insouciance found in the Democratic-Progressive Resistance, while the hard version likewise wants to advocate for those groups it deems victims—and according to Fonte, *"immigrant groups [are] designated as victims."*[80]

---

79   Cf. *Seeing Things Politically*, p. 146 & *A World beyond Politics?*, p. 30.
80   After naked partisan political calculation, these two reenforcing ideologies are the most plausible explanation for the Biden administration's criminal malfeasance when it comes to the security of our southern border.

Moreover, there is no need for the Resistance worldview to be entirely monolithic. Its members are more likely to share "family traits." Hence the need to move in somewhat concentric circles from the Democratic Party to progressives and progressivisms, as I have done. But it is quite striking what they share in common, as expressed in their common *condemnatory* terms and language: "illegitimate"; "racist, xenophobic, Islamophobic"; "fascist"; and worse. These bespeak a binary worldview, by way of violated moral-political criteria.

Therefore (to repeat): it is important to recognize that it is not just Donald Trump's manifest personal faults and failings that are targeted: it is what he (imperfectly!) represents. He claims to speak for Americans marginalized by global neoliberalism and contemporary political correctness ("wokeness") and for the proposition that American politicians should attend to the American people first and even aspire to American greatness *as America*. These views are anathema to the Resistance. To investigate why is arguably the most urgent civic task today, as one considers America's present political divisions and its possible futures. John Fonte saw in them a "coming civil war."

Chapter Fourteen

After this lengthy treatment of the Resistance-in-opposition, it is time for a brief interlude, before bringing our reflections to a conclusion by considering what the Declaration has to say about identity politics-in-power. Above, I criticized Danielle Allen for inappropriately attempting to appropriate the Declaration for progressive ends. In this chapter, I turn to the Right and chastise a conservative for failing to take seriously the Declaration. The conservative in question is Harvard Law professor and well-known "common good constitutionalism" advocate, Adrian Vermeule. As my review shows, one has to wonder if he should be called a conservative at all in the American context, disdaining as he does both the Constitution and the Declaration.

HISTORICIZING CLASSICAL WISDOM (2022)

In the case of Adrian Vermeule's *Common Good Constitutionalism* one could say that the specialist's tail wags the disciplinary dog. Vermeule is the Ralph S. Tyler, Jr. Professor of Constitutional Law at Harvard Law School, specializing in administrative law. In less metaphorical terms, he is that not-infrequent (but still dismaying) figure, a Constitutional scholar who disdains his discipline's charter document. Instead of being a defender of "the formal Constitution," he is a proponent of what he calls "our small-c, operative constitutional order." The "operative constitution" has historically evolved and is now "executive-centered." Thanks to History, and to those who have gone along with It,

> the American small-c constitutional order has come to feature broad deference to legislatures on social and economic legislation and broad delegations from legislatures to the executive. In operation, moreover, lawmaking is effectively centered mainly on executive government, divided in complicated ways between the presidency and the administrative agencies (including both executive agencies and independent agencies).

In other words, History has produced the Administrative State.[81] Vermeule aims to justify it with his Common Good Constitutionalism. Instead, he displays historicist supineness, tendentious scholarship, and political utopianism.

Vermeule's argument has four steps or components. First, he bows before History; secondly, he introduces a normative concept, "the Common Good," to justify what History has wrought; third, he critiques what he says are the two main interpretive alternatives contending today, progressive "living constitutionalism" and conservative "originalism"; and fourth, he claims that he is not grafting an alien branch on to our constitutional tree, but is returning to its original roots, which are to be found in an older tradition of legal and constitutional thinking.

---

81   It is helpful to capitalize "the Administrative State" to indicate the authority with which Vermeule invests it. One's eyes, then mind, should be arrested by the claims he makes on its behalf. The same is true for his appeal to history: "History" captures and conveys its authority. The same is true for "the Common Good."

Vermeule's Updated Classical Vision

Vermeule calls this older tradition *jus commune* legal theory, or "classical law" for short. It is a complex combination of morality and law, which includes "background commitments" to "the *jus gentium* (the law of nations or peoples) and the *jus naturale* (natural law)." Its chief contention is that law (and indeed all political action) ought to be oriented to the common good—legitimated and judged by it. Because "the classical law [was] the fundamental matrix for the thinking of the whole founding generation," "[t]he classical tradition should be explicitly recovered and adopted as the matrix within which American judges read our Constitution, our statutes, and our administrative law." Vermeule goes so far as to affirm that "if anything has a claim to capturing the 'original understanding' of the Constitution, this does. The classical law *is* the original understanding" (italics in the original). James Madison and John Marshall may beg to differ, but one would never know that from reading Vermeule.

It is not just the "American judges" mentioned above who should operate this way, but all public officials. If they do, America will "flourish" as a political community, its members' rights will be properly grounded (but also limited, sometimes severely, by their "ends" or purposes), and the manifold problems raised by a complex modern society will be effectively addressed. This importantly entails the provision of economic security and environmental health and safety. As a result, however, property rights will become a second-order reality and concern. *Kelo v. The City of New London* is a harbinger of "takings" to come. And based on his endorsement of past practice (see below), free speech too will be fair game for limitation and restriction.[82]

82 Given his endorsement of government-mandated lockdowns, vaccine mandates, and so forth, which included government suppres-

Nor will it only be America's Good that will be sought. The Common Good that Vermeule advocates embraces "the community of peoples and nations." American legislation, administration, and jurisprudence will have to be reoriented accordingly. Pope Francis's encyclical *Laudato Si'*, "On Care for Our Common Home," referenced twice by Vermeule, provides a sketch of the more expansive governmental vision and internationally oriented activity that it warrants.

Such is the vision Vermeule offers to the reader in lieu of anything purporting to be adherence to the Constitution with its superannuated principles of separation of powers, federalism, and limited government. Perhaps dazzled by his own radiant vision, Vermeule shows himself remarkably sanguine about Government's goodness and quite insouciant about the untoward possibilities inherent in such a Common Good-empowered State. His own endorsement of rights-ignoring vaccine mandates and draconian lockdowns is a hint of how far he thinks the State is authorized to go in the name of public health. Such policies caused an enormous loss of jobs and social mobility and created a set of second-class citizens, to say nothing of the abuse inflicted upon schoolchildren by politicians in cahoots with teachers' unions. One shudders to consider what policies he might endorse in the name of economic security, environmental protection, or public morality.

The Vermeulean Common Good is nothing if not *empowering*. Any serious concern that tyranny could operate in the name of the Common Good does not make an appearance in these pages. (In an earlier book, he derided such concerns as "Tyrannophobia.") Put another way, two things that his retrieval of the classical tradition does *not* include are recognition and provision for human

sion of dissenting scientific and journalistic voices (see the discovery of *Biden v. Missouri*), one wonders how much speech Vermeule would allow to be suppressed in the name of the Common Good?

fallibility and sinfulness, or for just plain lust for power. In other words, he is as ignorant of tyrannical idealism as of cynical realism.[83]

Historia Justificans

With equal insouciance, Vermeule declares that "[d]espite the high volume of chatter in originalist and libertarian circles, the federal government for all intents and purposes has acquired by prescription, over time, a *de facto* police power." *De facto* is of course not the same as *de jure*. Perhaps in other contexts, Vermeule would acknowledge the validity of the distinction. But not here. He does know (and acknowledges) that as late as 1870, the Supreme Court explicitly denied that the federal government constitutionally possesses the equivalent of the states' police powers. But over the course of three paragraphs, he lovingly sketches the erosion of that constitutional limit and the concomitant empowerment of the national government. History is once again a beneficent agent. At sketch's end, reprising a phrase employed above, he notes that "[o]ver time, the difference between state police power and federal enumerated powers became more theoretical than real." "Over time" does a lot of work in his argument. The passage of time and its solidification into History serves as a magic wand that waves away mounting constitutional scruples.

Aware that there might be something problematic in this historicist procedure, Vermeule provides a justifying "account": "I

83 One is reminded of Burke's insight into the tyrannical potentials and trajectory of the French National Assembly when he learned it was largely composed of lawyers, whose legal training and practice, absent political experience, malformed their minds for politics' complexities and conundra and of Tocqueville's analysis of a major Old Regime error in its intellectual class, the practice of ungrounded "literary politics."

offer an account that aims to put our constitutional order, including the administrative state, in its best possible light, given our whole history—not merely our most recent history." The Administrative State has happened, therefore it must be justified. Here "theory" provides its service to History. "This book is as much a work of memory and recovery as of theory." "[A]s of theory" means that theory is equally required to do the work of justification. This he finds in "the core theoretical insights and jurisprudential principles of the classical legal tradition," which center around and constantly repair to "the Common Good." According to Vermeule, this double light of theory and History "yields a better interpretation of the past and the present of our operative constitutional order" than anything else currently on offer.

The Expansive Common Good

According to Vermeule, the Administrative State is a Historically necessitated and justified "determination" of the Common Good. Before the "determination," however, we need the thing. Here, too, it turns out that History, both intellectual and actual, has played a decisive role in the (developing) understanding of the Common Good. In shorthand, one can summarize the development in terms of three names: Ulpian, the Roman jurist (170–223 (or 228) A. D.); Thomas Aquinas, the great medieval scholastic (1225–1274); and Giovanni Botero, the originator of "the *ragion di stato* tradition" in modern times (1544–1617); along with an amorphous authority, "modern conditions." It is true that the latter is more History than theory.

The modern contributor, Botero, proves decisive because of the specifications (additions?) he contributed. "The *ragion di stato* tradition . . . spoke of the *bonum commune* as comprising, more specifically, a triptych of 'justice, peace and abundance.'" According to Vermeule, "[t]his became . . . the standard list of the polity in which it is possible to live honestly, to do no harm to others, and to render to each his due" (the latter elements come from Ulpian). It's not clear from Vermeule's account, however, whether or how this seventeenth-century Spanish Catholic's concept impacted Anglo-Protestant or American jurisprudence. Be that as it may, they are used by him to directly justify "the administrative state": "the administrative state is today the main locus and vehicle for the provision of the goods of peace, justice, and abundance central to the classical theory."

To the list of proper names above, one must add Vermeule himself. The amorphous "modern conditions" need their own spelling-out and Vermeule takes it upon himself to "extrapolate [the *reason of state* triptych] to modern conditions to include various forms of *health, safety, and economic security*" (italics in the original). Like Topsy, the Common Good keeps growing. We saw above how far—Covid authoritarianism and *Laudato Si'* global environmental regulations—Vermeule is willing to go in its ever-grander Name.

It is true that Vermeule declares that "I also elicit from the tradition the key principles of *solidarity* and *subsidiarity*" (italics in the original). However, the top-down, or top-heavy, Administrative State takes clear precedence in his Historically-evolved American schema. As we saw above, it is armed by him with an expansive set of objectives to which it must attend and to which it can appeal in its ruling actions. Subsidiarity will always be at a decided disadvantage in a Common Good debate.

In summary, Vermeule largely ignores the most important works and constitutional thought of the framing generation, starting with Publius, John Marshall, and Joseph Story, and substitutes for them History's work, purportedly now justified by a grandiose conception of the Common Good. Committed to the latter, he brushes aside the sorts of questions, considerations, and caveats that made—and make—what used to be called "the genius" of our constitutional framework with its division of powers, federalism, and orientation to a complex political good as laid out in the Preamble to the Constitution. This complexity concludes on a high note with "the Blessings of Liberty to ourselves and our Posterity." Of this constitutional goal and promise, hardly a word from Vermeule.

Playing Cat-and-Mouse With Natural Rights

With unselfconscious irony, Vermeule begins his book with a ringing declaration that "American public law suffers from a terrible amnesia." He thus makes historical recollection and accuracy his initial criterion. Since what's sauce for the goose is sauce for the gander, it can and should be applied to him. As we indicated above, here he falls short, blinded by his commitments and agenda. As Peter Berkowitz put it in an earlier review, "Vermeule tenderly uncovers and dusts off lost treasures of our jurisprudential inheritance while scornfully burying other precious jewels and gems of our constitutional tradition."[84]

Aware of them, he wants to iron out tensions in the founding materials between what he calls an older *jus commune* view of law and a modern natural rights-based understanding. Among other things, the former envisaged political community in light of "the inherently political and social nature of man," a view Vermeule contrasts with one that is "more social-contractarian in its premises," that is, one that "tended to emphasize natural rights and saw human nature as intrinsically individualistic rather than social and political." To do so, he gives the former the whip-hand in their relationship and inflates it beyond its founding-era understanding and limits.

84 https://freebeacon.com/culture/too-good-to-be-true-the-virtues-and-vices-of-common-good-constitutionalism/.

Indeed, he initially goes well beyond smoothing out tensions, declaring (as we saw above) that "the classical law [was] the fundamental matrix for the thinking of the whole founding generation." To this claim, one should contrast Thomas West's detailed exposition of *The Political Theory of the American Founding* which argues for a thoroughgoing natural rights foundation; Michael Zuckert's notion of "the natural rights republic" as an "amalgam" of elements with a natural rights core; and Robert Kraynak's construal of "The American Founding as Blended Scotch" containing a number of intellectual sources, including Protestantism. All of these accounts, while disagreeing among themselves, expose the tendentiousness of Vermeule's opening claim about the founding era.

Things, however, are more complicated (as they can be with Vermeule). He eventually acknowledges the centrality of natural rights in the founding period. He does so, however, in a less-than-conspicuous way, in an endnote. Citing the Catholic integralist Edmund Waldstein, O. Cist., he concurs that "the [founding] era was already in transition from a classical conception of law and rights to a modern liberal conception." This acknowledgment relegated to an endnote indicates that Vermeule is aware of an important shift in legal and constitutional thinking occurring in founding-era America, but one that he doesn't want to think through. *Novus ordo seclorum* isn't allowed to enter the discussion, much less set the tone.

But even this belated acknowledgment doesn't fully capture Vermeule on this important point, which concerns the moral-political "ends" of the new American republic (see just below). When it serves his purposes, he acknowledges and even trumpets the founding-era natural rights form of political community. His go-to instance is blasphemy laws. Here was a conspicuous limit on freedom of speech in the founding era (and well beyond.) In this connection, Vermeule cites a scholar, Jud Campbell, who "shows that judicial review was sharply limited, not as a contingent matter, but by the very terms of the natural law and natural rights theories themselves." Campbell writes:

> [W]hether inherently limited by natural law or quali-
> fied by an imagined social contract, retained natural
> rights were circumscribed by political authority to pur-
> sue the general welfare.

Here Vermeule would leave the impression that the two great sources of political morality in founding-era America, natural law and natural rights, led to the same conclusion, that "the general welfare," capaciously understood, was the lodestar of American politics and jurisprudence. Well, yes and no. Here we return to a topic raised and discussed much earlier in Chapter Two.

The Declaration's Dialectic of "Ends"

It is telling that Vermeule mentions the Declaration of Independence only once in his book (and that by-the-bye) and the original state constitutions likewise only once and in passing. These documents, however, as authoritative "expressions of the American mind" (Jefferson's phrase), should be given considerable weight in whatever account one gives of the founding generation's political and legal fundamentals. They show the centrality of natural ("unalienable") rights in the founding-era conception of the common good and, therefore, a certain dialectic between the claims of natural rights-liberty and proposals of the common good.

The Declaration nicely illustrates these dual commitments and dialectic. In words that were once well-known, it declares that

> We hold these truths to be self-evident, that all men
> are created equal, that they are endowed by their Cre-
> ator with certain unalienable Rights, that among these

are Life, Liberty and the pursuit of Happiness.—That to secure these rights, Governments are instituted among Men, deriving their just powers from the consent of the governed,—That whenever any Form of Government becomes destructive of these ends, it is the Right of the People to alter or to abolish it, and to institute new Government, laying its foundation on such principles and organizing its powers in such form, as to them shall seem most likely to effect their Safety and Happiness.

A rich passage, I note but two things in it which are relevant to our discussion. First, it contains a duality and dialectic of ends. The aim of Government begins with "to secure these [individual] unalienable rights," but it ends with "their [the People's] Safety and Happiness," the alpha and the omega of a political community. Individual rights, popular safety, and popular happiness—all are within Government's competence and concern. This trio sets up a dialectical triangle that will constantly be debated by a sovereign People and its representatives. In times of danger, individual rights may be circumscribed. In times of plenty, it may deem that a National Endowment for the Arts would contribute to their Happiness. At any time, it may judge that public education in civic rights and duties may conduce to the protection of rights and to the common weal. And so on. With this trio of ends, the broad terms of American debate are set and unleash a constant back-and-forth among partisans of each. Welcome to democratic life in the fledgling republic.

Declaration Justice

Having noted this dialectical structure, one must also note that rights—unalienable rights—come first. They have a primacy and a divinely granted ("endowed by their Creator") independence. In

America, one starts with individual rights. Founding-era Americans would therefore both agree and disagree with Vermeule on the nature of rights. First, the agreement:

> In this tradition, "rights" very much exist, but they are not defined in the essentially individualist, autonomy-based, and libertarian fashion today.

George Will's reading (to take a salient example) of the Declaration in *The Conservative Sensibility* is libertarian wish-fulfillment and a betrayal of the founding era's substantive understanding of rights, which are grounded in nature and God, correlated to duties, and their employment measured by publicly shared moral criteria.[85]

They would therefore agree and disagree with Vermeule's introduction of justice into the discussion. He continues:

> Instead "rights" are corollaries of justice, which is the constant aim of giving each man his due.

Justice as "giving each man his due" would ring true for the original Americans. But what's due to each is, primarily, the protection and free exercise of his natural rights. For Vermeule, on the other hand, "the common good" (with the dictates of Ulpian's "legal justice" and Thomas' precepts of "natural law" at its core) is the primary criterion of justice, which determines (and limits) what is due, not an independent notion of natural rights. As we said above, he wants to iron out a tension, rather than live dialectically with a variety of American commitments. His return to the founding is therefore more agenda-driven than dispassionate scholarship. Berkowitz was right.

85 See Chapters One and Three above and Chapter Fifteen ("The Declaration's Principled We") below.

A second point: In the Declaration, the structure of "Government" is a matter of foundational "principles" and "powers" organized in "formal" ways. More expansively, fundamental principles of governmental aims ("these ends," "Safety and Happiness") and construction (e.g., the subordination of military to civilian rule, the priority of legislative to executive power), delegated and organized "powers," and constitutional "forms and formalities" (to use Harvey C. Mansfield Jr.'s phrase[86])— are some of the essential features of the Declaration's blueprint for constitutional construction. However, rather than following the Declaration's lead to the Constitution to see how the Framers and sovereign American People determined these matters after experimenting with the Articles of Confederation, Vermeule, as we also said above, largely ignores the most important works and constitutional thought of the framing generation and substitutes for them History's work, now justified by a grandiose conception of the Common Good. He is thus that oxymoron, a classical historicist. As for me, I prefer my classics, as well as my Constitution, straight.

86 *America's Constitutional Soul* (Johns Hopkins University Press, 1993).

Chapter Fifteen

I did not pen an essay in 2020, the summer of the "mostly peaceful protests" over the death of George Floyd—accompanied by a host of grievances, demands, violence, looting, destruction of property, and killings. Like a good deal of the country, I watched in horror at the eruption of mayhem and violence directed against America, its present, its past, and its principles. That meant that the next essay I penned took place with a new President and a new administration in place. With President Biden and his administration, identity politics was in power. Now the "resistance" shoe was on another foot. What guidance could the Declaration give to those who wish to resist identity politics-in-power?

THE DECLARATION'S PRINCIPLED "WE" (2021)

After a year's hiatus, I am back with my annual "Declaration and Us" reflection. My dual purpose remains the same: to commemorate the Declaration and to indicate its ongoing relevance. The two purposes go together. To commemorate the document fitly, one must take seriously its teachings. Among the most basic of its lessons is that even in contentious times such as ours, reason can discern and judge what is going on, and it can guide action, individual and collective. It can discern and judge, when it combines permanent principles of political judgment with a grasp of the relevant "Facts" of the situation. More specifically, in their combined light it can discern the enemy, or enemies, of freedom. At the extreme, it can discern in his (or their) actions a "Design" to establish despotism. On the basis of such assessments, it can judge that it is time—indeed, morally imperative—to act in freedom's defense. While the document itself does not provide a plan of action, its own example contains important lessons about speaking and acting on behalf of freedom. After all, the Declaration itself is a grand speech which is a grand action—it is an argument and an act.

I write this six months into a new presidential administration, the Biden administration. Two of the new chief executive's initial statements of aims sent mixed messages. He vowed to be a uniter of the country and to be the most progressive President ever. His subsequent deeds indicated which of the two to take seriously. A flurry of executive orders, a number of radically progressive nominees (Xavier Becerra, Kristen Clarke, Neera Tanden), mammoth spending bills that redefined the English language (and paid back supporters, Chicago-style), the mandating of divisive "diversity, inclusion, and equity" programs for all federal agencies, including the military, and the symbolic cementing of the cozy relationship between "Big Tech" and progressive politics with the appointment of Ron Klain as chief of staff[87]—in these actions the Biden administration flew its true colors and showed its transformative ambitions. Many other facts in this vein could be adduced—abortion extremism, collusion with legislative allies to abolish important

---

87 Just how cozy was revealed subsequently by the Twitter files published by Matt Taibbi, Bari Weiss, Michael Schellenberger, and others, and further put on record in the discovery in *Biden v. Missouri*. https://aaronkheriaty. substack.com/p/slaying-the-censorship-leviathan; https://www.nationalreview.com/news/1576737/?bypass_key=ZlJEdVFhRXluMUJQdnND-WWYvaGp0QT09OjpTbVpJYkRJM1dYWXlWVzV0YUROdVNWW kVkMFpxUVQwOQ%3D%3D?utm_source%3Demail&utm_medium =breaking&utm_campaign=newstrack&utm_term=33805836&utm_sour ce=Sailthru.

forms of ordered liberty, the memory-holing of the 1776 Commission—but the initial list is enough to indicate a "Design" on the part of the Biden administration.

On the Fourth of July, therefore, one could well ask, what would the Declaration have to say about this "designing" administration and its aims? Next year, with more "facts" or evidence, we will do so. This year, however, I would like to take things in a different direction. Stipulating that the Biden administration has a partisan ideological design on the country, of the sort I have laid out in previous chapters on the nature of progressive identity politics, I would like to turn my attention to what the Declaration has to teach about resisting such a design. One could call this a contribution to "True Resistance Studies." To do so, I will begin with the fundamental unit of the Declaration, what I call "the stout individual": the individual cognizant of God-given natural rights and formed in such a way that he or she is able and willing to assert and defend them before God and human beings. Then, I will segue to the necessary banding together of such individuals into a "we." The title of these reflections indicates that the "we" is my main focus and that I aim to stay largely (with two illustrative exceptions) at the level of principles. The reader is invited to make his or her own applications to their particular circumstances.

The First Line of Resistance

Perhaps the first lesson the Declaration of Independence imparts to us in our situation is contained in the title of the document itself. In the face of "designing" executives and their legislative enablers, one must declare oneself, one must declare one's independence. Here, "to declare one's independence" takes on a specific meaning. It means summoning the moral courage to stand up and speak out, to declare publicly and privately oneself against despotic designs, abusive power, and denials (and deniers) of God-given natural freedoms and our precious constitutional forms and liberties. To declare one's independence is to take a principled stand for principles of ordered liberty against their would-be despotic deniers.

Of course, to do so requires an individual of a certain sort. A close reading of the text would reveal his lineaments. Earlier (in "The Declaration and Thoughtful Citizenship" and "The Declaration's Civic Anthropology"), I provided some essential components. To recall a few: in the first essay, the figure of admirable humanity emerging from the text is principled and prudent, manly, a lover of liberty, capable of cooperation and sacrifice, and understands himself within in an estimable tradition of liberty. In the second essay, we saw that in the Declaration human equality and freedom are combined with significant ontological and moral content, they are not free-standing notions, they do not warrant human beings to make of themselves whatever they will. Rather, all three (equality, rights, and moral qualities) are based upon a determinate notion of human nature and all are placed before the divine Gaze and Judgment. In my view, this substantial figure would be a fine model for American civic education and a fine figure of humanity for philosophers to consider.

"We" in Three Lessons

Happily, as the example of the Declaration also shows, when one does one's human and civic duty and stands up, one discovers that one is not alone: there are like-minded others and "ones" together can form a "we." About this "we," the Declaration contains a number of lessons that are relevant to today's defense of liberty. I will discuss three.

The first pertains to the troubling fact that civic friends have to deal with civic enemies, with what we could call civic *frères ennemis*. Declaration British-Americans separated from the British government and people because of differences of principle resolvable only by revolutionary change. Today's Americans are arguably divided by even greater differences of principle concerning justice and human liberty. The Biden administration in particular embodies principles that are antithetical to those of the Declaration, starting with the injustice of making justice a matter of group-identity rather than individual merit and conduct. How to deal with these civic *frères ennemis* is a question to which the Declaration makes succinct, but significant, contributions. It is important to bring them to light.

The second lesson recognizes that a resistant "we" contains leaders and led. There is a division of talents and roles that both must recognize in order for effective resistance. A third lesson unites the two groups in a common *ressourcement* in a history of the practice of ordered liberty. Our annual reading of the Declaration participates in that lesson.

Civic *Frères Ennemis*

The first lesson is admittedly a hard one: the "we" which *includes* people on the basis of shared principles also perforce *excludes* others on principle as well. Principles entail "principled differences"; they separate as well as unite. As George Santayana wrote: "I have drawn my circle of friends and included you out." This is the situation in which the signers of the Declaration found themselves as members of the British Commonwealth; this is arguably the situation in which those devoted to ordered liberty under God find themselves today vis-à-vis the current administration and its allies.

What to do with such civic *frères ennemis* is a thorny question. To begin with, the Declaration realistically shows the *terminus ad quem* of such principled disagreements. It is separation, sometimes violent. Inherent in disagreement over fundamental principles, separation can be rationally foreseen and predicted, although its realization or averting is left to human prudence and choice (with accident playing its role). In 1776, one party of "we's" judged that matters had come to a head. We will get an initial indication of where things stand in 2024, but the battle over principles will no doubt continue thereafter.

The Declaration is not without lessons for us on this score as well, i.e., of waging civil battle civilly. In its fourth part, it alludes to "repeated" efforts of "humble petition" of king and parliament and "reminders" and "appeals" to shared bonds—natural, civil, and civilizational—with fellow citizens standing apart from the fray. These passages indicate important dispositions to have and kinds of overtures to make to civic *frères ennemis* and to by-standing third parties. They provide elements of a possible path to civic reconciliation. They also remind us of the necessary tempering of spirited indignation toward fellow citizens (if not toward their designs). However, one must also note that along with the reminders and appeals went—and go—"warnings" and "conjurings." As always, it remains to prudence to make these determinations. Prudence in turn requires manly firmness so as not to shrink from the task.

With its characteristic realism, the Declaration also lets us know that our best efforts may fail. It even indicates what the complex meaning of "failure" is. *Our* failure would be a failure to offer arguments on behalf of liberty, theirs would be the failure to even engage the arguments for ordered liberty. The final failure would be to have the designing party declare that it will only be satisfied with the full implementation of its views. That final failure would entail that the terrible options before the lovers of liberty are yielding to despotism, peaceful separation, or the horrors of civil war. To avert this terrible choice is their sincere desire, hence an important reason why they band together. The second and third lessons bear upon important characteristics of this banding.

The Few and the Many

The Declaration shows that the resistant "we" is not a homogenous or an undifferentiated mass; it contains structures and leaders and led. This division of roles is important to their success and important for us to recognize. A political philosopher might say that this is "the political problem" *in nuce*, insofar as the political problem is the problem of effectively conjoining the few and the many. The Declaration expresses a special moment in this eternal drama and its American reconciliation merits celebration and reflection. It also bears repeating, if in different circumstances and ways, today.

A self-descriptive phrase on the part of the signatories of the Declaration summarizes the American achievement: "We, therefore, the Representatives of the united States of America, in General Congress, Assembled, do … in the Name, and by Authority of the good People of these Colonies, solemnly publish and declare…." Note the progression from a "We" that begins as select and few broadens to include an entire "People." In turn, the few, the signatories who pledge their "sacred honor," here speak and act on behalf of—they are authorized by—the many, "the good People of these Colonies."

The whole formed here is expressly political, with the express tie between the two parts being representation. It is structured by longtime and more recent political structures: "Colonies," "States," and "General Congress." With the last item, the Declaration invites us to expand our own thinking when it comes to structures and forms, reminding us that a free people can be creative with the forms it adopts. In recalling this, I am not advocating changing the Constitution. Rather, I am pointing to the current need for new institutions and ways to bring resistant-minded individuals together. (Benjamin Franklin's famous saying comes to mind.) In today's circumstances, the enemies of freedom and equality under the law possess many of the commanding heights of the economy and culture, as well as the executive branch. Creativity and new forms are imperative.

Happily, I do see such initiatives pullulating on the contemporary scene. They indicate that our Tocquevillian genius for association continues to be fecund. When it is, it is because of the initiative of some and the support of many. One example of what I have in mind occurred recently in Southlake, Texas and has given heart to many. It involved the all-important battle ground of public education and brought to the fore a new champion of reason and liberty, Hannah Smith.[88] Based on what we see in many school districts today, where women are leading the countercharge against the scourge of indoctrination in injustice, race hatred, and gender madness, one can hope that a new generation of Abigail Adamses is on the rise.[89]

An Estimable History of Manly Firmness

The connecting of contemporary and founding heroines is not rhetorical on my part. I continue to follow the Declaration's lead, albeit expansively. In its third part, which is the recitation of "injuries and usurpations" on the part (largely) of the king and (partly) of his abettors in parliament, the Declaration recalls its own predecessors. Speaking of the king, its authors recall that "He has dissolved Representative Houses repeatedly, for opposing with manly firmness his invasions on the rights of the people." The "Representatives" we met earlier are following in their predecessors' footsteps. A tradition of "manly firmness" is thus recognized and continued. As the examples of Abigail Adams and Hannah Smith suggest, one

88 https://latterdaysaintmag.com/a-stunning-pushback-against-critical-race-theory-in-schools/.
89 https://nypost.com/2021/06/13/american-moms-are-standing-up-to-critical-race-theory-devine/.

can take the adjective "seriously, but not literally." And as a fitting conclusion to my admittedly spirited reading of the Declaration on this Fourth of July 2021, all of us—male and female, young and old—could be encouraged by their examples to continue this quintessential American tradition.

Chapter Sixteen

In 2022, I kept a promise made the year before and turned the Declaration's searching eye on the Biden administration. Once again, the title of the essay indicated its thesis and agenda.

GOVERNMENT UNDER JUDGMENT
(2022)

It is again time for my annual Fourth of July "Declaration and Us" essay. In this series of essays, I try to honor the day by taking the document seriously. From the start of the series in 2014, I have taken my bearings from Jefferson's famous phrase (in a letter to Richard Henry Lee) that the Declaration is "an expression of the American mind." My guiding questions have been: How did that mind look at the world? How would that mind look at *our* world?

This year is no different. What is different is the topic. How can we discern grave political evil? For as it happens, the American mind expressed in the Declaration is neither an ostrich nor a Pollyanna. Quite the contrary, it is on the lookout for political "evils." Specifically, it would have us be on the alert for "injuries and usurpations" on the part of government, or for their close cousins, "abuses and usurpations." Most ominously, it would have us be on the lookout for "designs" on the part of government agents and their allies to subject a free People to the greatest political evil, "absolute Despotism." As the founding document of the United States of America, the Declaration stands as a warning to subsequent American governments that they exist under judgment.

They are under human judgment, but they are also under divine judgment, as the concluding paragraph of the document indicates. In appealing to "the Supreme Judge of the world," the signers of the Declaration applied a distinct sort of "religious test" to themselves and to King George's government, which he failed by systematically violating the duties of his office. To be sure, this test was different from the religious tests subsequently banned by the Constitution. Both, however, go together in the American founding dispensation. While the Constitution enshrines religious liberty, the Creator's moral-political standards are inscribed in the Declaration's normative vision for politics and government. So too are conscientious appeals to His verdict on conduct that violates them.

To be sure, the Declaration also observes a certain natural conservatism and patience on the part of the People in the face of even egregious governmental misconduct. And it counsels "prudence" in dealing with errant government. But repeated misconduct can add up to "a long train of injuries and usurpations" that finally calls for recognition and response. And if the People are slow to grasp the trajectory of events, leaders can step forward and, by bringing principles to bear on marshalled facts, help focus and form the popular mind. This is an important part of what "the Representatives" of "the good People of these Colonies" are doing in the Declaration itself.

Last year (in "The Declaration's Principled 'We'"), I wrote about the instruction and example the Declaration provide to those who wish to band together against the designs of a misguided administration bent on manifold mischief. This year, I wish to turn to the logically prior topic, the criteria of judgment the Declaration puts forth to discern advancing injustice and despotism. The Declaration does so in two places principally. The first is what I have earlier called "the principles of politics" found in the second part of the document. This part lays out the "ends" of rightful government and the principles of its construction; both can be employed as criteria to judge governmental officials and their deeds. To what ends do their actions tend? Are they acting within the bounds of their offices? More substantively, does government in all its branches—legislative, executive, and judicial— aim at the principal object of government, which is to protect the inalienable rights of its citizens? These are direct questions that go to the heart of the matter.

Thus, from the Declaration's point of view, all governmental policies of "affirmative action" understood and practiced as quotas are deeply wrong. Even more so are initiatives of group-identity politics that promote or suppress individuals in the name of largely concocted group categories. In another vein, the byzantine apparatus that goes by the name of "the administrative state" is a prime candidate for violation of the principles of the Declaration, distorting by usurping all three branches of government. The administrative state violates these principles in two major ways: placing legislative, executive, and judicial powers in a fourth set of hands and by being largely unaccountable. Because of these features, it makes itself an attractive target for capture by corporate interests or ideologues who can thus circumvent democratic will and accountability.[90] The Supreme Court's usurpation of state police powers in the name of its own concocted jurisprudence of "privacy" and "autonomy" is another major area of Declaration (and Constitutional) concern because of its negative impact on federalism and the moral life of the country. Insofar as that jurisprudence is in place, the phrase "our robed masters" continues to be chillingly accurate. Recent decisions by the Court, however,

90   Philip Hamburger, *Is Administrative Law Unlawful* (University of Chicago, 2014); *The Administrative Threat* (Encounter Books, 2017). John Marini, *Unmasking the Administrative State* (Encounter Books, 2019).

have given some hope of a course correction by the errant institution.[91]

Finally, given the Declaration's keen interest in the executive's abuse of the military and administration (see below), it would look with horror on the weaponizing of entire departments by partisan administrators. Whatever happened to Lois Lerner, former head of the IRS, who deliberately targeted conservative groups? While she got off scot-free, her spirit seems to have migrated to the bodies of Merrick Garland and Christopher Wray, having passed through those of James Comey and John Brennan. A two-tiered system of justice, such as these gentlemen preside over, is no system of equal justice; even more ominous is when the scales of justice are deliberately turned against political opponents—pro-lifers, traditional Catholics, protesting mothers, and former Presidents—as is the case with the Wray FBI and the Garland DOJ.

Particulars, Patterns, and Principles

The second pertinent passage is the lengthy list of "injuries and usurpations" perpetrated by the king and his allies in Parliament laid out in part three of the Declaration. Because it lists specific abuses, injuries, and usurpations on the part of the king and (eventually) Parliament, it is particularly relevant to our topic, for several reasons. It draws our attention to specifics, which in turn imply or refer to principles. That combination is itself a lesson for political judgment. Particulars, patterns, and principles must be brought and thought together when considering the conduct and character of government. In this respect, the Declaration is both a specimen

91 The *Dobbs v. Jackson Women's Health* decision, together with *Students for Fair Admissions v. Harvard* (2023), hopefully signal a Supreme Court self-correction. Justice Thomas' concurrence indicated directions in which it should go.

and a model of political reasoning. Having founded America, it can continue to form Americans in their political judgment. In what follows, therefore, I will survey the list in order to tease out principles, then venture a few applications to our government as presently constituted. The reader, of course, is welcome to agree, disagree, or add to my applications.

"Injuries and Usurpations"

The full list of grievances contains twenty-seven items, eighteen committed by the king and nine by Parliament. They divide into five parts and progress in a crescendo of malfeasance to a necessary conclusion.

The first seven items bear upon the king's—the executive power's—relationship to legislative power, specifically the legislatures of the Colonies. The legislative power of government and its well-working is the first concern of the mind surveying the American past and present. In social contract theory that priority makes perfect sense, since legislative power is the first power of government discussed by Locke, for example. In language more consonant with the Declaration itself, however, legislative precedence is warranted as the chief organ of the self-government of a free people. To attack the rights of legislatures is not just to deny the norm of common rules equally applied, but to attack a sovereign people in its character as self-governing. This is the opening section's chief and underlying concern. It is so important to Declaration thinking that it will recur later as Parliament's chief misdeed.

After the legislature, the next two items deal with the executive's relationship to the judiciary. Thus, within the first nine items, we have the three great powers of liberal government. Implicit in the fact that charges of executive wrongdoing are again being leveled are standards of the proper relationship between it and the judicial power. The two invoked here are adequate provision for the judicial protection of a people and, connected to that, the independence of the judiciary. "He has obstructed the Administration of Justice, by refusing his Assent to Laws for establishing Judiciary powers" and "He has made Judges dependent on his Will alone, for the tenure of their offices, and the amount and payment of their salaries." With respect to the king's wrongdoing, there are sins of omission and sins of commission. In both cases, one detects an executive intent on bending the judicial power to his will. These are actions of an aspiring tyrant.

"Swarms" and "Standing Armies"

Next come three very disconcerting "works" of the executive in areas that in principle are central to his office (administration and defense), but in practice betray an ominous "Design." The list is short enough to cite.

> He has erected a multitude of New Offices, and sent hither swarms of Officers to Harass our people, and eat out their substance. He has kept among us, in times of peace, Standing Armies without the Consent of our legislatures. He has affected to render the Military Independent of and superior to the Civil Power.

While the erection of new offices may in the abstract be justified or innocuous, its real purpose becomes clear when officeholders proceed to harass and impoverish those they should serve. The biblical term "swarms" is particularly telling here, as it indicates excessive numbers bent on nuisance and spoliation. The term indicates executive governance gone terribly awry.

This *a fortiori* is the case with the two subsequent items, which consider the situation in which the executive has used its authority over military forces as though peacetime were wartime[92] and "the Military" was solely its instrument to wield. Here basic principles of non-threatening, non-tyrannical, government have been flouted. Following the earlier trend, the legislative contributions to free government have been overridden. This is already quite alarming, but there is even worse executive action to recount.

Complicit Parliament

Before continuing in this belligerent vein, however, the Declaration lists nine usurpations on the part of Parliament. Parliament was enlisted as the king's ally in violating the "constitution" that had organized political relations between the colonies and the metropole. An opening statement prepares the specific charges to follow: "He has combined with others [Parliament] to subject us to a jurisdiction foreign to our constitution, and unacknowledged by our laws; giving his Assent to their Acts of pretended Legislation." Then follow nine specific instances of Parliament's "pretended Legislation." The ninth returns to the first seven items of the list and strikes at the heart of American self-government. Their "pretended Legislation" aimed at "suspending our own Legislatures, and declaring themselves invested with power to legislate for us in all cases whatsoever." Here was a direct, and definitive, assault on colonial self-government.

92 This phrase reminds of the discussion of Aaron Kheriaty's book in Chapter Three, where he informed us of two decades of "war-gaming" against dissenters to government vaccination policy. Since it is the government's (and their allies') own term, one can use it without being liable to the accusation of hyperbole.

The Bellicose State of Nature

The fifth and last section of the indictments returns to the monarch and brings to a bloody culmination his belligerent actions. Withdrawing his protection from the colonies, he has introduced a state of nature between them and himself. In keeping with the worst possibilities of that condition, he has waged war against them. His conduct of this war has included "transporting large Armies of foreign Mercenaries to compleat the works of death, desolation and tyranny," "exciting domestic insurrections amongst us," and enlisting Indian tribes to wage war against "all ages, sexes, and conditions." In a characteristic act of tyranny, he has compelled citizens captured at sea to bear arms against their country and their civic brethren. Classical wisdom long ago recognized that sowing discord among citizens and pitting them against one another is a characteristic *modus operandi* of the tyrant. King George confirms this ancient wisdom.

Today

This last point can be a jumping off point to today. From day one, the appointments and flurry of executive orders of the present administration made it clear that it is all-in when it comes to advancing identity politics. This form of politics deliberately sows discord among the citizenry. It conceptualizes the American people in terms of opposing groups and pits them against each other. In so doing, it violates the Declaration's fundamental conception of justice, which centers on the rights of individuals, their talents and skills, their individual characters and deeds. It should constantly be called out as the ugly face that truly systematic injustice displays today. Patriotic representatives should make a habit of ending each speech, whether in Congress or on the stump, with *politica identica delenda est.*

Given the Declaration's keen interest in the king's abuse of the military and administration, it would look with horror on the weaponizing of departments by partisan chief administrators alluded to above. Disconcerting realities in this vein have come to light repeatedly in recent years. Informed citizens reasonably worry that the leaders of the IRS, FBI, and DOJ are fundamentally untrustworthy and are willing to betray their public mission for the sake of serving the political interests of particular parties and persons. Worse, given their mounting pile of coverups, lies, and illegal activity, they have even more incentive to prevaricate and dig in. The battle against these malfeasant leaders and the institutional corruption they have perpetuated will be one of the defining contests in (and for) the Republic going forward. In a similar vein, in response to Covid-19, governmental officials (Anthony Fauci, Francis Collins, Rochelle Walensky) and departments (the CDC, NIH, NIAID, FDA) grossly abused their powers and conspired with allies in media and Big Pharma to squelch legitimate scientific and policy debate, further legitimizing citizens' concerns about abusive administrative power. If these developments are not stoutly resisted and effectively rolled back, "dissenting" scientists, independent journalists, public good civic organizations, and "mere" alternative voices will continue to be targeted for harassment and worse by their political opponents in federal and state agencies. A Great Reckoning of the Covid years, no matter how unlikely or implausible, is another *sine qua non* of republican health.[93]

---

93 In my review of Aaron Kheriaty's book, I highlight steps that he says need to be taken at the federal level: https://lawliberty.org/book-review/confronting-pandemic-tyranny/. Likewise, the Supreme Court's eventual decision in *Biden v. Missouri* will be a decisive juncture in the battle for freedom and democracy.

Military Demoralization and Debacles

The ongoing implementation of identity politics in our armed services brings the two preceding points together. Enforced wokeness has predictably demoralized our military, accelerated retirements, and exacerbated the decline in recruitment. These results confirm the folly of making the military an ideological plaything, more concerned about social engineering than the waging of war. The debacle of the withdrawal from Afghanistan also displayed the military incompetence of our current regime, while calling into question the military's current leadership. Not a single general officer resigned in the wake of this national humiliation. The toadying General Milley who betrayed his oath by going beyond his President's back is the poster child for this deep corruption in our highest military ranks. Ideology and careerism make for a toxic brew.

Conclusion

Ideology and political power are even more dangerous, however. Sooner or later, they are destructive of the liberties and self-government of a free people.

Almost two hundred and fifty years ago, the American colonists considered the king's conduct and aims and reflected on them in light of their right to and desire for self-government. They determined they had no future with him, so their future had to be without him. Today, we need to ask similar questions about the current administration and its many allies and accomplices. These days, alas, the lessons of the Declaration concerning political evil are daily confirmed. We urgently need to take them to heart, in the principled, prudent, and manly way they are conveyed in our remarkable founding document.

A VERY BRIEF CONCLUSION

The foregoing essay, "Government Under Judgment," is a natural and fitting conclusion to this collection of essays. While there is more—much more!—that could be extracted from the Declaration, and events will continue to unfold and occur, the chief lesson that I wished to impart in these essays has been more than adequately conveyed. According to the Declaration, in America government exists under judgment. It is the people's creation and servant, not our master. Of course, the Declaration (not to mention Publius) knows full well that a secure and prosperous people needs government. But not just any sort of government. The need for government is not an excuse for bad government or, *a fortiori*, despotic government. With its principles, and by its example, it shows how to assess administrations and governments and to respond appropriately, that is, with principled prudence and "manly firmness."

In these essays I have tried to make good this claim by expositing the text and applying it to us. This is a traditional practice, sometimes called *explicatio et applicatio*. Originally applied to Scripture, it makes sense that one could apply it to the text Pauline Maier called "America's Scripture." Not a preacher, but an American citizen and student of political philosophy, these have been my contemporary glosses on that founding text. If they have convincingly indicated to the reader something of its riches and continued relevance, I would be more than pleased.

Paul Seaton
April 18, 2024

APPENDIX:
THE DECLARATION OF INDEPENDENCE

In Congress, July 4, 1776

The unanimous Declaration of the thirteen united States of America, When in the Course of human events, it becomes nec-essary for one people to dissolve the political bands which have connected them with another, and to assume among the powers of the earth, the separate and equal station to which the Laws of Nature and of Nature's God entitle them, a decent respect to the opinions of mankind requires that they should declare the causes which impel them to the separation.

We hold these truths to be self-evident, that all men are created equal, that they are endowed by their Creator with certain unalien-able Rights, that among these are Life, Liberty and the pursuit of Happiness. —That to secure these rights, Governments are insti-tuted among Men, deriving their just powers from the consent of the governed, —That whenever any Form of Government becomes destructive of these ends, it is the Right of the People to alter or to abolish it, and to institute new Government, laying its foundation on such principles and organizing its powers in such form, as to them shall seem most likely to effect their Safety and Happiness. Prudence, indeed, will dictate that Governments long established should not be changed for light and transient causes; and accord-ingly all experience hath shewn, that mankind are more disposed to suffer, while evils are sufferable, than to right themselves by abol-ishing the forms to which they are accustomed. But when a long train of abuses and usurpations, pursuing invariably the same

Object evinces a design to reduce them under absolute Despotism, it is their right, it is their duty, to throw off such Government, and to provide new Guards for their future security. —Such has been the patient sufferance of these Colonies; and such is now the necessity which constrains them to alter their former Systems of Government. The history of the present King of Great Britain is a history of repeated injuries and usurpations, all having in direct object the establishment of an absolute Tyranny over these States. To prove this, let Facts be submitted to a candid world.

He has refused his Assent to Laws, the most wholesome and necessary for the public good.

He has forbidden his Governors to pass Laws of immediate and pressing importance, unless suspended in their operation till his Assent should be obtained; and when so suspended, he has utterly neglected to attend to them.

He has refused to pass other Laws for the accommodation of large districts of people, unless those people would relinquish the right of Representation in the Legislature, a right inestimable to them and formidable to tyrants only.

He has called together legislative bodies at places unusual, uncomfortable, and distant from the depository of their public Records, for the sole purpose of fatiguing them into compliance with his measures.

He has dissolved Representative Houses repeatedly, for opposing with manly firmness his invasions on the rights of the people.

He has refused for a long time, after such dissolutions, to cause others to be elected; whereby the Legislative powers, incapable of

Annihilation, have returned to the People at large for their exercise; the State remaining in the mean time exposed to all the dangers of invasion from without, and convulsions within.

He has endeavoured to prevent the population of these States; for that purpose obstructing the Laws for Naturalization of Foreigners; refusing to pass others to encourage their migrations hither, and raising the conditions of new Appropriations of Lands.

He has obstructed the Administration of Justice, by refusing his Assent to Laws for establishing Judiciary powers.

He has made Judges dependent on his Will alone, for the tenure of their offices, and the amount and payment of their salaries.

He has erected a multitude of New Offices, and sent hither swarms of Officers to harass our people, and eat out their substance.

He has kept among us, in times of peace, Standing Armies without the Consent of our legislatures.

He has affected to render the Military independent of and superior to the Civil power.

He has combined with others to subject us to a jurisdiction foreign to our constitution, and unacknowledged by our laws; giving his Assent to their Acts of pretended Legislation:

For Quartering large bodies of armed troops among us:

For protecting them, by a mock Trial, from punishment for any Murders which they should commit on the Inhabitants of these States:

For cutting off our Trade with all parts of the world:

For imposing Taxes on us without our Consent:

For depriving us in many cases, of the benefits of Trial by Jury:

For transporting us beyond Seas to be tried for pretended offences:

For abolishing the free System of English Laws in a neighbouring Province, establishing therein an Arbitrary government, and enlarging its Boundaries so as to render it at once an example and fit instrument for introducing the same absolute rule into these Colonies:

For taking away our Charters, abolishing our most valuable Laws, and altering fundamentally the Forms of our Governments:

For suspending our own Legislatures, and declaring themselves invested with power to legislate for us in all cases whatsoever.

He has abdicated Government here, by declaring us out of his Protection and waging War against us.

He has plundered our seas, ravaged our Coasts, burnt our towns, and destroyed the lives of our people.

He is at this time transporting large Armies of foreign Mercenaries to compleat the works of death, desolation and tyranny, already begun with circumstances of Cruelty & perfidy scarcely paralleled in the most barbarous ages, and totally unworthy the Head of a civilized nation.

He has constrained our fellow Citizens taken Captive on the high Seas to bear Arms against their Country, to become the executioners of their friends and Brethren, or to fall themselves by their Hands.

He has excited domestic insurrections amongst us, and has endeavoured to bring on the inhabitants of our frontiers, the merciless Indian Savages, whose known rule of warfare, is an undistinguished destruction of all ages, sexes and conditions.

In every stage of these Oppressions We have Petitioned for Redress in the most humble terms: Our repeated Petitions have been answered only by repeated injury. A Prince whose character is thus marked by every act which may define a Tyrant, is unfit to be the ruler of a free people.

Nor have We been wanting in attentions to our British brethren. We have warned them from time to time of attempts by their legislature to extend an unwarrantable jurisdiction over us. We have reminded them of the circumstances of our emigration and settlement here. We have appealed to their native justice and magnanimity, and we have conjured them by the ties of our common kindred to disavow these usurpations, which, would inevitably interrupt our connections and correspondence. They too have been deaf to the voice of justice and of consanguinity. We must, therefore, acquiesce in the necessity, which denounces our Separation, and hold them, as we hold the rest of mankind, Enemies in War, in Peace Friends.

We, therefore, the Representatives of the united States of America, in General Congress, Assembled, appealing to the Supreme Judge of the world for the rectitude of our intentions, do, in the Name, and by Authority of the good People of these Colonies, solemnly publish and declare, That these United Colonies are, and of Right ought to be Free and Independent

States; that they are Absolved from all Allegiance to the British Crown, and that all political connection between them and the State of Great Britain, is and ought to be totally dissolved; and that as Free and Independent States, they have full Power to levy War, conclude Peace, contract Alliances, establish Commerce, and to do all other Acts and Things which Independent States may of right do. And for the support of this Declaration, with a firm reliance on the protection of divine Providence, we mutually pledge to each other our Lives, our Fortunes and our sacred Honor.

Georgia
Button Gwinnett
Lyman Hall
George Walton

North Carolina
William Hooper
Joseph Hewes
John Penn

South Carolina
Edward Rutledge
Thomas Heyward, Jr.
Thomas Lynch, Jr.
Arthur Middleton

Massachusetts
John Hancock

Maryland
Samuel Chase
William Paca

Thomas Stone
Charles Carroll of Carrollton

Virginia
George Wythe
Richard Henry Lee
Thomas Jefferson
Benjamin Harrison
Thomas Nelson, Jr.
Francis Lightfoot Lee
Carter Braxton

Pennsylvania
Robert Morris
Benjamin Rush
Benjamin Franklin
John Morton
George Clymer
James Smith
George Taylor
James Wilson
George Ross

Delaware
Caesar Rodney
George Read
Thomas McKean

New York
William Floyd
Philip Livingston
Francis Lewis
Lewis Morris

New Jersey
Richard Stockton
John Witherspoon
Francis Hopkinson
John Hart
Abraham Clark

New Hampshire
Josiah Bartlett
William Whipple

Massachusetts
Samuel Adams
John Adams
Robert Treat Paine
Elbridge Gerry

Rhode Island
Stephen Hopkins
William Ellery

Connecticut
Roger Sherman
Samuel Huntington
William Williams
Oliver Wolcott

New Hampshire
Matthew Thornton